1 MONTH OF FREE READING

at

www.ForgottenBooks.com

By purchasing this book you are eligible for one month membership to ForgottenBooks.com, giving you unlimited access to our entire collection of over 1,000,000 titles via our web site and mobile apps.

To claim your free month visit:

www.forgottenbooks.com/free796140

* Offer is valid for 45 days from date of purchase. Terms and conditions apply.

ISBN 978-0-483-88556-1
PIBN 10796140

This book is a reproduction of an important historical work. Forgotten Books uses state-of-the-art technology to digitally reconstruct the work, preserving the original format whilst repairing imperfections present in the aged copy. In rare cases, an imperfection in the original, such as a blemish or missing page, may be replicated in our edition. We do, however, repair the vast majority of imperfections successfully; any imperfections that remain are intentionally left to preserve the state of such historical works.

Forgotten Books is a registered trademark of FB &c Ltd.
Copyright © 2018 FB &c Ltd.
FB &c Ltd, Dalton House, 60 Windsor Avenue, London, SW19 2RR.
Company number 08720141. Registered in England and Wales.

For support please visit www.forgottenbooks.com

LONDON
PRINTED BY S. AND R. BENTLEY, DORSET STREET

GUESSES AT TRUTH

BY

TWO BROTHERS.

———

THE SECOND VOLUME.

———

LONDON:
PUBLISHED FOR JOHN TAYLOR,
WATERLOO PLACE,
BY JAMES DUNCAN, PATERNOSTER ROW,
AND SOLD BY J. A. HESSEY, FLEET STREET,
AND HATCHARD AND SON, PICCADILLY.
1827.

Hardly do we guess áright at things that are upon earth, and with labour do we find the things that are before us: but the things that are in heaven who hath searched out? *Wisdom of Solomon,* ix. 16.

Ὤναξ οὗ τὸ μαντεῖόν ἐστι τὸ ἐν Δελφοῖς οὔτε λέγει οὔτε κρύπτει ἀλλὰ σημαίνει.
Heraclitus ap. Plutarch. de Pyth. orac. p. 404.

Vasta ut plurimum solent esse quæ inania: solida contrahuntur maxime, et in parvo sita sunt.
Bacon. Inst. Magn. Præf.

GUESSES AT TRUTH.

It may seem inconsistent with some foregoing observations, to quarrel with a jest; nor would I, so long as it pretends not to be something else. But wit will not keep; jokes to be good ought to be fresh; the airy particles which give them flavour, evaporate as they pass from mouth to mouth, and they grow so stale and vapid and mawkish that every man of taste nauseates them. Hence, to continue current, they must have a nominal as well as a real value: they must appear at least to be more than mere jests; they must represent some truth, or mimic it. In this manner what was originally perhaps thrown off in harmless gaiety, being repeated as a proverb and retailed as a maxim, may become mischievous; inasmuch as Wit, which delights in heightening and deepening all contrasts, is nearly allied to that sophistry which thrives by perplexing and confounding all relations: and after a saying has thus been abused, one is loth to sully one's lips with it. Of such a kind is that vulgarest of street-walking vulgarisms, that smart, pert, tawdry, trickish cheat: *Why should I do anything for Posterity? Posterity has done nothing for me.*

The sophistry here is so shallow, one should be unwilling to expose it, did not continual experience teach us that the shallows cause many more wrecks than the depths. People may grumble about dark and deep mysteries; it is not among them that men make shipwreck of their souls; it is on some jagged rock, or flat sandbank near the shore. The saying I have cited, begins with utterly perverting the ideas of duty and moral obligation. Several words expressive of these ideas have been derived from words expressive of debt : *duty* itself for instance is that which is *due* ; and I *ought*, as every one knows, is only the preterite of 'I owe;' although according to the usual practice, where a word has at once two forms and a double signification, of dividing the property between them, *ought* is now used exclusively in the moral sense; and that even as a present, since the affinity of sound connected the old present *owe* more closely with the other preterite *owed*: so important did the distinction of meaning appear, that grammar was violated to preserve it. All this is convenient enough, so long as the original notion is allowed to lie in the back-ground, not thrust obtrusively forward and unseasonably substituted for the derivative. But it cannot supplant, without overthrowing it. To assert that a duty nowise differs from a debt in the commercial sense of the word, that what I ought I owe, just like a guinea which I have borrowed, and that unless I have incurred such a debt, unless I have actually borrowed the guinea, I am under no moral obligation; an assertion of this kind is no less irrational than to insist that the water when it springs out of the earth, filtered, and purified and impregnated by the substances through which it has passed, is still nothing but snow and rain, because once perchance it may have been so. In one way of regarding it indeed, the primitive meaning is a very just one : whatever I ought to do, I *owe*: I owe it to the God who made me and gave me the power of doing it. I owe it, as a tree owes or ought to bring forth fruit after its kind, in obedience to the law of my nature, and in discharge of my debt for whatever gifts I may have received. Here too our language has most philosophically hit the truth : whatever I owe or own, or possess, I owe; whatever is my own, is owed : *own* also is only another form of the participle *owed*, from which, as from *ought*, a new present has arisen. Therefore to say I owe no duty to such a man, because I have received nothing from him, is rank nonsense and perverse confusion. I owe him, whatever I can do for him; and I owe it, because I can do it: that is of course, when it interferes not with other obligations; but the secondary question need not be considered here.

Now this may be called an idle piece of work about what all the world knows. Would that it were! But that proverb is too often quoted, alas! not irrelevantly; and when one casts one's eyes around, it would almost seem as if everybody were acting upon it. At least one very remarkable characteristic of our age, is the absolute want of any care for posterity. We have well nigh forfeited all claim to that noble description of man, as looking before and after. Short-sighted people, it has been observed, increase daily: short-thoughted people have multiplied far more rapidly. Providence has been contracted into prudence: so, having squeezed up the name, we think ourselves bound at least proportionably, to contract the span and scope of the faculty. Indeed if there be any Gospel precept to the accomplishment of which we have recently made any considerable approach, it must be that of taking no thought for tomorrow: only I am afraid one should have to read *after tomorrow*; the truth being that we think so much about the morrow, we can find no thought to spare for the day beyond it, or even for the day behind it. Look at the buildings of the men in ancient times, their temples and their amphitheatres, their minsters and their castles: were they not also, like their writings, κτήματα ἐς ἀεί; while our houses are already many of them biennials; and if we mind well what we are about, we may at last contrive to make them ephemeral. We are become the purveyors and jackals of Destruction, bargaining however that we shall have our share in the booty: whereas our ancestors wrought in a magnanimous spirit of rivalry with Nature; or in kindly fellowship with her at other times, as when they planted, choosing out her trees of longest life, the oak, the chesnut, the yew, the elm, trees which it does us good to behold, while we muse on the many generations of our forefathers whose eyes have reposed within the same leafy bays. Amongst them are trees by gazing on which Milton or Shakspeare may have enriched his imagination with visions of beauty, trees under the shade of which Philip Sidney or the Black Prince may have slumbered, trees which may have witnessed the wars between the Norman, the Saxon, and the Dane. Now oaks, thank God, cannot be made to grow faster: it would take from the countryman his most capacious measure of Time, who creeps over them so softly that his progress is scarcely discernible, except by some new beauty ever springing up beneath his gentle beneficent tread. What we can do however to be beforehand with Death, we do: we plant the trees of quickest growth, and such as promise the speediest return, trees which we may ourselves hope to cut down and to put the money into our own pockets; thus degrading that most liberal and farsighted and least selfish employment, in which we most intimately consult and commune with Nature, and subordinate our wayward wilfulness to her unerring will, into a vulgar and mercenary trade. The commonest trees in our modern plantations are the horse-chesnut, the Scotch elm, the sycamore, firs of various kinds, above all the larch, that apt type of the age, brittle, thin, perking, premature, outgrowing, upstart, monotonous, with no massiness of limb, no variety of outline, no prominences and recesses for the lights and shadows to play in. It has little beauty save of the lowest kind, mere symmetry, the beauty which most captivates all such imaginations as have not strength enough to combine and harmonize a greater diversity of elements : if any other trees come near it, even this vanishes, and it becomes dry and rugged, and careless about all other things, if it can but lift its head above its neighbours : when you have seen one larch, you have seen all; for every deviation is a deformity; nay, when you have seen a single side of one : for however you may change your point of view, it still presents the same insubstantial self-satisfied appearance, as if Nature for once had meant to shew that she could have kept pace with man even in poverty of invention. Then we have our companies and associations, in which brocage is only the first step toward breakage, and which fall to pieces, so to say, long before they are put together. Who can tell how many of them existed yesterday? or how many will exist tomorrow? you might as easily count the swallows on their passage, or the worms that crawl out after a shower. There is no petty corporation, which will not outlive them all: it was established in an age when men knew rather better how to fix the holdfasts of society. Our ancestors legislated: we write treatises on legislation. Without knowing how, they made laws which have lived for centuries, and promise to live for centuries to come; we know how, at least we do not doubt it; and yet one seldom expects that any law enacted during the last session will escape without either revision or repeal the next; beyond which, it would be invidious to ask, how many members of our legislature have projected their minds. If the law of the Medes and Persians was justly characterized as that which altereth not, the law of England in our times may no less justly be characterized as that which altereth. Consider too the governments now in being throughout Europe: are not the oldest the most likely to endure? and of the new ones, those where, as in Wirtemberg, innovation has had the wisdom to content itself with being renovation? As for our literature, a large portion of it has taken the name of journal, and nine-tenths of the rest might without the slightest impropriety. Few authors expect to outlive the season, any more than partridges; many meet their end on the first day; hardly two or three in a large covey see a second winter, hardly one a third. It matters not to them: the reputation of the day is so clamorous and deafening, they cannot listen amidst it to catch the distant voice of Fame. In short we seem to have made up our minds that we will leave no *souvenir* to Posterity, except our debts. Posterity will be even with us, and will reward us as we deserve; by forgetting that such a selfish, voracious, trivial, inch-eyed, minute-minded generation ever trod the earth. Nor will the earth remind them of us: those monuments which she displays with the fondest pride as memorials of what her children have done, are the monuments of those whom she has long since taken into her bosom; and she does not seem likely to find any new favorites soon.

This indictment may be deemed overdrawn by those who make their boast of their age, as of their cravat; I only ask whether the several counts are not true. But to turn to the sophistical proverb, let me take it by the horns. You, whoever you are that make use of it, assert that you owe nothing to Posterity, because, as you assert, Posterity has done nothing for you. You are ignorant then of your greatest earthly benefactor. Posterity has cast her shadow before, and you are at this moment reposing underneath it. Whatever good, whatever pleasure, whatever comfort you possess, you owe mainly to Posterity. The heroic deeds that were done by the men of former times, the great works that were wrought, the great fabrics that were raised by them, their mounds and embankments against the powers of evil, their drains to carry off mischief, the wide plains they redeemed from the overflowings of barbarism, the countless fields they inclosed and husbanded for good to grow and thrive in: for whom was all this achieved, but for Posterity? Except for Posterity, it never would have been achieved: except for Posterity, except for the vital magnetic consciousness- that while men perish man survives, the only principle of prudent conduct must have been, *let us eat and drink for tomorrow- we die.* We toil, because we die not, because we live to reap the harvest of our toil, if not in ourselves, yet in Posterity. All this, I say, was done for Posterity: not for you, or for me, or for your next neighbour, or for any single generation, but for Posterity; that dim, majestic, multitudinous idea, with the broad earth for its throne, and illimitable time for the period of its dominion, with the sweet light of Glory ever radiating from its face, and the sweet voice of Fame ever gushing from its choral lips. To this idea they brought their most precious offerings, and laid them at its feet : this invisible light cheered them, when they would otherwise have desponded amid the gloom ; this inaudible voice often comforted and heartened them, when they were on the eve of abandoning their task. That same light will cheer you too, if you but look curiously for it; that same voice will comfort you, if you hearken for it diligently ; and you will then incur a far goodlier and prouder obligation to Posterity; an obligation you will rejoice to acknowledge. But even as you are now, inhabiting a civilized land, eating the bread and drinking the wine of social life, your obligations to Posterity are inestimable ; you are warmed by its reflected light; and unless you go forth into the woods, and strip yourself, body and heart and mind, of all you have and feel and know, and turn a homeless, heartless, reckless, thoughtless, godless savage, Posterity will still have done far more for you than the service of your whole life can repay.

I know not how to close these observations more fitly, than by reminding the reader of the last words written by Lady Jane Grey on the table-book which she gave to the constable of the Tower, when about to lead her to the scaffold. They may serve to put him in mind of the greatest among all the great blessings which he owes to Posterity, the most precious of all his heir-looms, the virtues of his ancestors. That meek and heroic lady thus expressed what had upheld her, and what has in like manner upheld many others: *If my fault deserves punishment, my youth at least and my imprudence are worthy of excuse; and God and Posterity will shew me favour.* U.

Sic vos non vobis, said the old poet somewhat querulously; and many since have echoed his complaint. For it is not the privilege of bees and birds and sheep and oxen only: it is the common lot of mankind; and the greatest men have the greatest share in it. But is it indeed so grievous? Ask a mother. U.

———

One saves oneself much pain, by taking pains; much trouble, by taking trouble. U.

———

The indolent are seldom the strong, either bodily or mentally. It is the man with only one talent, who wraps it up in a napkin and buries it; while they who have more, make increase in proportion to what they have received. Indeed few men have ever hoarded money, who have not some time or other felt the want of it. U.

———

Let not your field or your mind lie fallow too long: they will produce a large crop of weeds; and weeds are much readier to take root than to leave it.' The most profitable husbandry, that which best works the land without exhausting it, is by a change of crops. Longhi, the great engraver of Raphael's lovely *Marriage of the Virgin*, told me that he made it a rule always to have two prints in hand, and that turning from one to the other was the only relaxation he needed. For relaxation means loosening, not untying; and when you have loosened your faculties, you may soon tighten them again: but if you let them lie on the ground, they get entangled and knotted, until it is often no easy task to bring them into order.   U.

When you pluck up a weed, take it up by the root: when you pluck out a vice, shew no mercy; extirpate it. If you only tear off the head of the weed, for the sake of making your garden look neat, ere long it will come up again, with a new head sprouting from every fragment of the root. Can there be a more complete illustration of the parable in which the unclean spirit after going out of the man, takes with him seven other spirits worse than himself, and returns into his house from whence he came out? The weed even finds the place empty, swept, and garnished: but worse than vain is all labour of which the sole aim is a decorous outward seemliness; and the last state of that garden is worse than the first. A relapse is still more dangerous in a spiritual disease than in a bodily. U.

What is the great blessing of a very forward state of civilization? That there are no highwaymen; and... and.... and plenty of pickpockets.

Perhaps this may hold in other senses besides the literal. U.

In former times people were put into the stocks; and, as we learn from Shakspeare, there was at least one honest man amongst them. Now-a-days people put into the stocks; and... but Mercury in more than one of his capacities forbids my divulging the secrets of his wards. υ.

Men who feed on nothing but meat, contract a gross habit of body: Men who think of nothing but money, contract a gross habit of mind: or usurers have been scandalously belied.
υ.

The wealthy Jews scarcely intermarry but among themselves. Would that this were true morally and spiritually, as well as physically!
υ.

The division of labour is the application of *Divide et Impera* to matter; and in this sense alone ought that maxim ever to have been uttered. In its common acceptation it is grossly and mischievously false. The first principle of politic wisdom is the exact reverse: *unite and rule*: let that which was scattered be gathered together, and let order be the cement of union. Assimilation is the great mean of organic growth; not only in particular bodies, but in states: and except as facilitating or preparatory to combination, division is altogether inefficient and good for nothing. You cut up your ox into joints, in order that you may the more easily dress them: you cut up your sirloin into morsels, in order that you may swallow and digest them: in both instances the latter is the important process, and without it the former is of no use. Yet politicians have seldom learnt this: they usually stop short in the slaughter-house: they hack and hew and chop, and then they carve and mince; and then, when the pieces are at their smallest, they look out for another body to serve after the same fashion; marvelling all the while why their strength does not increase prodigiously.

And even with reference to matter, one must beware of carrying the principle too far: even here it ought to be secondary rather than primary. As secondary, it will procure for us everything that appertains to man's legitimate sway over the world he is placed in: if this leaves us discontented, and we aim at establishing a despotism, we may set it up as primary; and we shall then fall under that curse from which, through the blessing of God, no despot has ever been exempt, of becoming our slave's slave. Unless the mist which the thought calls up into my eyes deceive me, there are symptoms of such a destiny to be detected in England at this day: I refer not to the events of the last twelvemonth: that were to confound the disease with the pain which warns us of it, and which, if we heed it, may lead us to seek for a remedy before it is too late. u.

Everybody has laughed at the old woman killing her goose that lay the golden eggs. All our master-manufacturers have laughed at it: all our political economists have laughed at it: England herself, had she a mouth to laugh with, would distend that mouth into a grin at it. For they tell you, laughter makes people forget themselves. U.

It is rather droll that the unquenchable laugh of the Homeric Gods should be at their brother who has turned himself into a mechanic. The gods of this generation would deem him the only sensible person amongst them all: in him alone can they find nothing to laugh, or, as their way rather is, to sneer at. No matter that he fell from Heaven: Heaven must be a very idle useless place, if no manufactories are to be found there. No matter that he limps: what is the use of walking straight, or having two legs of the same length? Man's business is to sit and work, not to walk about like an automaton that has nothing better to do.

Homer however has made him some amends, by giving him a Grace for his wife; thus intimating that even the mechanical arts, of which beauty is not the animating principle, as it is in the cycle that Apollo presides over, ought still to be wedded to beauty.

Oh! there's not much sense in that. Beauty is of no use. But you know, Homer was a poor blind heathen. U.

There has been much controversy about the true reading of the Good Friday cry. The sticklers for accuracy and meaning in little things, insist at their peril that it ought to be: *One a penny, two for twopence, hot cross-buns!* On the other hand the pure lovers of antiquity, who love a thing all the better for its being somewhat unreasonable, turn with disdain from anything so punily arithmetical, and uphold the authority of all the oldest women in favour of *One a penny, two a penny, hot cross-buns!* Mr. Bentham has decided the dispute: for he, I am credibly informed, is in the practice of walking about crying, *One a penny, two a penny, constitutions!*　　　　　　　　　　　τ.

Whatsoever you do, do thoroughly: never divide your forces, as poor silly Argus did, and lock one half of them up in sleep, while the other half are to watch at their post: let the whole man be seen in every action of your life: do it with all your heart and with all your soul and with all your mind. And tell me not that I am profaning sacred words. If you were duly conscious of God's omnipresence, you would not make so frivolous an objection.

But are we then to do evil with all our heart, and with all our soul, and with all our mind? It is impossible. Were there no half-doers, there would be no evil-doers. It is the want of unity in our nature, that causes the want of integrity in our conduct. The father of evil has outwitted us: he was crafty enough to anticipate the arch maxim of our statecraft: he divided us, and thereby made us his slaves.   U.

Scarcely anybody has a whole heart. A few may have some three-quarters of one; a good many, half; still more, about a quarter; the chief part of the world, a little bit of one. No human being, I trust, has ever yet lived without any heart; for his senses without feelings leave man the nethermost of animals; although in some it may have been like the figs one sees on a tree late in autumn, a starveling, with a kind of promise that it will come to something; but the winter intervenes and nips it.

By heart, I mean the complex of all such feelings as look outward, whatever may be their object, whether spiritual or sensuous, whether inanimate or animate; and I believe I only go along with common usage, in excluding self-love from the heart. For self-love is not a part of it, but its disease, preying upon it, and ossifying it as far as it reaches over it; and nothing but self-love is the cause why our hearts are only fragments and little more than splinters and shivers of what they ought to be: it is that, instead of loving ourselves in others, in God and his world, and our brother men, we love ourselves in distinction and separation from them, and therefore in opposition to them; that, instead of finding our chief happiness in the utmost expansion of our feelings, we shut them up within our own breasts, where they waste and crumble and moulder and rot.   U.

There is only one thing which people cannot endure to hear.

Falsehood?—O no! there is not much harm in that.

Flattery?—The sweetest thing in the world; only pray don't over-sugar it.

Nonsense?—How could one get through one's time without it?

Reason?—I have nothing to say for it.   U.

An honoured friend is fond of asking, *Don't you know the pleasure of finding one thing, when you are looking for another?* And verily few pleasures are sprightlier and more enlivening. It is satisfactory to meet with what you are seeking; but still sweeter is the surprise of lighting on something unsought, that appears as it were to answer a lurking yet indistinct unuttered wish, and to gratify it ere it excites it. Is it not just the same, when you have been awaiting somebody, and another friend comes up to you instead? you shake hands with him more heartily than you would otherwise; and your spirits seem on tiptoe to welcome him. Nor are intellectual searches less privileged.

When you let your faculties go a wool-gathering indeed, they bring back nothing besides wool. But if you set to work in right earnest, and diligently trace some dark question among the mazes of ancient learning, though you may still perhaps miss it, you will find abundant diversion and entertainment, and many things, it is likely, more profitable and instructive than what you had fixed your heart on. And still more certainly, should we embark in a vessel of speculation, duly rigged and trimmed, and fitted out with all needful implements of knowledge, and thus voyage into the yet undiscovered hemisphere of thought, although we may not fall in with the gold mines or reach the Eldorado we dream of, we shall yet gain things of higher worth and of more diffusive utility, even as Ralegh did when he brought home the potato. For while in active life the result very seldom comes up to our expectations, in speculative life it almost always surpasses them.

U.

It has often been asserted that to give is more delightful than to receive. I doubt it. Do you feel more pleasure in giving your dog a bone, or in his coming and licking your hand? Is not her child's smile the mother's ample and most precious reward? Much of the pleasure in the mere act of giving, consists in the anticipation of the return; while every gift we receive is a token of love, the one thing for which the heart hungers insatiably; of man's love, if it be the gift of man; of God's love, if it be the gift of God.

Surely the poet feels a far loftier and purer rapture at those thoughts which his genius breathes into him, than at anything his conscious understanding under order of his will can manufacture.

No! said a man of understanding: it is impossible for you to derive pleasure from anything except the consciousness of your own deserts, from being quite sure that what you have done is your own doing.

"Very well: then pray dismount and walk through that ditch, while my horse carries me over it. I shall not grudge you the satisfaction of having waded across the mire, even though you should enhance it and make the feat still more your own, by taking off your shoes and stockings, lest they should share in your merit. For my own part I always feel steadier and more comfortable when I am leaning on something stronger and mightier than myself."

I call that operation miraculous, wherein the moral predominates over the physical more perceptibly than we are wont to find it. That all the laws of nature are intellectual and spiritual, that the phenomena of the universe are only the outward forms of the workings of these laws, and no more the laws themselves than a block from Portsmouth is, I will not say the block-machine, but the steam-engine, or perhaps the steam which gives the machinery life and motion; all this is evident to a considerate mind. When a philosopher then calls a miracle a suspension or an alteration of the laws of nature, I cannot understand him; except indeed on the supposition that he is talking loosely, and cheating himself, or us, with words. Yet if the laws of nature are to be introduced at all into a statement of the difficulty, *suspension* and *alteration,* bad as they may be, are clearly better and less unphilosophical expressions than *violation,* Hume's term, which begs the question at starting.

But if we mend the definition, and describe a miracle to be such a new and unaccountable appearance in an object of common note as cannot have been produced by ordinary human agency; the objector will find it hard to deduce from such strangeness the incredibility of the fact asserted; until by comprehending the laws of nature in their full extent, he has ascertained with exactness all their possible phases of operation. What you are startled by as contrary to the laws of nature, may be only the phenomenon which under the particular circumstances those laws are framed to present; like the unforeseen changes in a great firework, which from a fountain becomes a ship first perhaps, and then a temple of glory. Could you demonstrate the reverse, you might on your own principles establish the impossibility of the miracle: till you can, you have no pretext for rejecting the evidence of the phenomenon, as contradicting laws of which in fact you know next to nothing. The aloe, they say, blows once in a quarter of a century: supposing the earth to be the aloe, why should not the miracle be its flower? But for our immersion in sense which stupefies and blinds us, we should rather wonder that it appears so seldom. To say nothing of the obstinate misgivings at the extent of evil, the triumphs of brute force, the desolation of innocence, the sufferings of goodness, which excited such deep questionings among the best and wisest heathens; almost every thing supernatural, providential, and extraordinary in works of fiction, and indeed the whole notion of poetical justice, points out that such is the appetite of our minds.

If however a philosopher abides by the first definition of a miracle, as a suspension of the laws of nature, he ought to discern in it only a new object to be answered by so wonderful and spirit-stirring an event. That which we esteem desirable to authenticate Christianity, will be welcome to him, as it disproves Fate, and thus tends to keep men from deifying Nature, by shewing that the succession of operations designated under that name, as it was first ordained by God's wisdom, so continues ever subject to

God's will, being the result neither of chance nor of necessity, but an order in a double sense, of regularity, and also of appointment.

It has been argued that man cannot conceive any notion of God, because what comprehends must be greater than that which is comprehended. Yes! just as that pane of glass is greater than the cluster of stars you see through it; just as the binding of that Shakspeare is greater than the spirit it incloses. υ.

The seventh day has been specially hallowed : is that a reason for unhallowing the other six? A large portion of literature in every Christian country must be exclusively religious : is that a reason for altogether excluding religion from the remainder? And yet the press brings forth volumes without number, which you can only infer to be written by a Christian, from its being clear that they are not written by the believer in any other religion. Were Christianity diffused as it ought to be through the nation, circulating through all our actions and amalgamated with all our thoughts, this would not be. Whatever is current among a Christian people, ought to bear the distinct effigy of its king. Not however that it belongs to religion to be impertinently obtrusive: this is no more a sign of its depth or sincerity, than it would be a sign of your wealth to keep chinking your few guineas in every body's ears: a practice which on the contrary would lead the shrewder to divine that he who makes so much of a little, can have but little to make much of. υ.

———

The lame stamp: the deaf scream. υ.

———

The art of saying nothing is often as difficult

for those who have something to say, as the art of saying something is to those who have nothing.

If you pull up your window a little, it is far likelier to give you a cold or rheumatism or stiff neck, than if you throw it wide open; and the chance of any bad consequence becomes still less, if you go out into the air and let it act on you equally from every side. Is it not just the same with knowledge? Do not those who are exposed to a draught of it blowing on them through a crevice, usually grow stiff-necked? When you open the windows of the mind therefore, open them as widely as you can: open them and let the soul send forth its messengers to explore the state of the earth. Although the unquiet raven may fly to and fro, and the home-loving dove may return once disheartened; yet if the dove, that emblem of all kindly affections, goes forth a second time, she will bring back the olive-leaf of peace: for *charity*, when it is indeed such, and has the patience and perseverance of true charity, *never faileth*. Nay, if you have the power, draw forth the spirit from its dark cell, and bathe it in knowledge as in an atmosphere: let it strip itself of all its habits and plunge in; as soon as it comes out it will resume them. Let the butterfly, by which ancient philosophy typified the soul, emancipate itself from its chrysalis and take wing: the readiest way to clear the head of maggots, which sleepy brains always breed, is by such a metempsychosis. The best, indeed the only method of guarding against the mischiefs which may ensue from teaching men a little, is to teach them more. Knowledge is the true spear of Achilles: nothing but itself can heal the wounds it may have inflicted. u.

The ideal aim and end in a perfect scheme of education, so far as concerns the intellectual part of man, is to produce a classical and catholic mind; classical from the refinement, the justness, and the orderliness of all its perceptions; catholic from the range of its comprehension, as well as from the cordial affectionate welcome and acknowledgement with which it receives and entertains every form of existence. Such a spirit will venerate all things, yet nothing will enslave it: thus is it the direct antipode to the *liberal* spirit now in vogue; for of the latter it is not exaggeration to say that it venerates nothing, yet is the servilest of slaves to every shifting gust, tossing about amid that heap of dead leaves which a misplaced courtesy terms public opinion.

The foregoing definition is a sufficient answer to the advocates of professional education. U.

The first object of education is to shape and discipline man, the second to teach him. You must build the house, before you furnish it. The communication and developement of power is of infinitely greater importance than the communication and infusion of knowledge; even as it is more wholesome and beneficial to give a person a good appetite and a good digestion, than to cram him with food however choice or nutritive. This proposition is so evident that I should not have repeated it here, unless the line of argument pursued in most of the recent discussions on education, had seemed to imply that it is forgotten. The problem considered in them has been, how to convey the greatest quantity of knowledge in the least time; and not, as it ought to have been, in what way are good and able men, or, to speak more precisely, good and able Englishmen, to be trained, with the greatest likelihood of success. I say *good and able Englishmen:* because every useful system of education must accord with the spirit of the nation to be educated. True, it should promote and help on that spirit; but the only method of doing so, is to go along with it: if you take another road, you will affect it very little; if you pull it the contrary way, you will hardly help it on.

Here however we find a new verification of the truth which Bacon after his custom has uttered in all its naked universality: for here too do knowledge and power coincide. It is by the judicious communication of knowledge that the faculties of the mind are to be elicited and nourished: in the very act of tilling the ground the seed is also sown. U.

Is it as a memento of the first offence, or as a punishment for it, or out of pure spite for having been unable to resist the tempter, that man ever since has set his heart on keeping woman in ignorance? How successful his endeavours have been in some instances, the following conversation will shew.

What are beef-steaks, mamma? said a pretty miss in her teens to her mother, who had locked up her own and her daughter's understanding with their silk gowns, through fear lest some chance spot might soil them irremediably.

Fy? don't talk about them, Imoinda; things which people eat at inns.

But do pray tell me how they make them, dear mamma?

I don't know anything about them, my sweet darling; but I suppose they grow.

This darkness on matters of housewifery may perhaps be unrivalled; but it would be easy to find parallels on subjects of almost equal importance.

Knowing men know little: teach them more, and they will know how little. u.

The ignorant man is ignorant of his own ignorance: the wise man is aware of his. This perhaps is the main difference between them. u.

To know the hight of a mountain, one must climb it. u.

A. (Everybody knows A: he is as common an article as the indefinite article itself; and he seems to resemble it in being unattached to the soil: he is always to be found on stage-coaches, in steam-packets, in travellers' rooms at inns, and in every other place of resort for such as think that Cain was a gainer by becoming a vagabond. He is a whimsical medley: disgusted with every thing strange, yet always running from place to place; longing for companions if alone, and when he has got them as uneasy amongst them as a fish among his comrades in a net; very fond of home, whenever he is away from it; assuring you that his servants are the best in the universe, provided they are too far off for him to swear at them; always out of his element, or, as the phrase is, always in the wrong box, or, like the weights in a balance, always in the empty scale; and yet getting on well enough through the crowd from keeping his arms ever folded, and making up for his incapacity of pleasure by the redundance of his self-complacency.) What will become of the world, if it goes on for the next fifty years at the same rate it has gone on for the last fifty?

B. It must go on faster still; its velocity must increase at every step: for I suppose you mean that it is going downward.

A. Downward! How can that be? Is not every thing improving? The world must be going upward; if ups and downs have any thing to do with the matter.

B. People seldom go very fast up hill, especially where the hill is a long one: the horses would soon be blown.

A. We shall have done with horses soon; and when we are drawn by steam, the faster we drive it the livelier it will become. So that a four-horse power is worth a dozen horses.

B. Without question; particularly in point of beauty and safety. You are sure then that the world is improving?

A. Perfectly sure: are we not driving twelve miles an hour, where fifty years ago we should not have driven six?

B. This certainly proves that stage-coaches are better, or at least that they travel faster.

A. Well, sir! stage-coaches are the best part of the world. How should I have seen every thing in the world, if it was not for stage-coaches?

B. Have you then really seen every thing in the world? You must have a well-stocked head.

A. To be sure: I have got it all in there: if you like to try me, you will find me as good as a road-book.

B. Still I cannot help doubting what you say. There are some tiny parts of the world, all Asia for instance, and all Africa, and almost all if not all America, and the bigger half of Europe, in which nothing like a stage-coach ever set wheel.

A. Who cares about such outlandish holes? By the world I mean England, the only bit of it worth a farthing. Once indeed I took a trip across the water; but the moment I landed I put my handkerchief to my nose, and did not take it away till I was aboard again. How can any Christian live in a country where one's hands must be always keeping guard before one's nostrils? I have heard say that the French language "is constructed upon stinks;" and sure enough they have plenty of ground to build it on.

B. Perhaps something might be said in their favour; only I am much more anxious just now to see the bottom of our first question: hitherto we have only muddled it by our stirring. The world then which has improved so prodigiously, consists in the first place of stage-coaches, and next of England.

A. Right, sir. What have you to say to that now?

B. Did you ever hear of Penelope's web?

A. No: what is she? a sort of spider?

B. She was the wife of Ulysses.

A. And what had she to do with a web? and what can her web have to do with the world?

B. You must let me take a run before I jump.

She used to spin it every day, and to unravel it every night.

A. The greater fool she. Had I been her husband, I would have taught her better housewifery; she should have left spinning to the Jennies. But I suppose, sir, it must have been before Sir Richard Arkwright's time.

B. Her husband was far from home; and this was her way of spending her time during the ten years of his absence.

A. Why, it was not worse than reading and writing. But ten years! there can have been no stage-coaches running in those days.

B. He was on the sea.

A. No matter: it is all one: he ought to have had a steam-boat. But how does all this concern the world's growing better or worse?

B. It sometimes seems to me as if the world were, like Penelope, in a state of widowhood, divorced and separated from her lord; and I fancy then that like her she is whiling away the sorrowful and unprofitable time in weaving and unravelling a web which can never be finished. Now and then comes a short interval of daylight, during which she sets all her faculties at work, and appears to be or conceives that she is approaching to something like a completion of her task; when darkness comes over her, or a new whim lays hold on her, and she undoes all she has been doing, to begin the next morning after a new fashion.

A. But did not Penelope ever finish her web?

B. Yes; when her enemies, pretending to be her lovers and suitors, forced her. I hope this is not to be the destiny of the world: when her web is spun out, God grant that it may not be at the instigation of the devil.

A. There is no fear of that. The devil would never make people comfortable: on the contrary I am sure he would have everybody as uncomfortable as himself. Now all the improvements in England are making people more and more comfortable every day.

B. Be it so: I will allow it for argument's sake; although for my part, if I wanted to ruin a person, body and soul, my bait should be what we call comforts. However let that pass. Are all orders of society equally or anywise proportionably sharers in this increase of comforts?

A. I can't go quite so far as to say that.

B. Is the advance in morality equal or anywise proportionable to the advance in luxury?

A. I am afraid the judges and gaolers and Jack Ketch to boot would cry *No.*

B. Are we in fine become at all better morally, at all kinder, more charitable, honester, more orderly, more temperate, chaster, more obedient, more dutiful, more pious, during these last wonderful fifty years.

A. Somehow I never thought of all this; and

now you put the question to me, I am not the man to say *yes* to it. All the old people tell me men have grown worse; and for myself, I certainly do not find so much kindness in other places, as I used to find thirty years past in my father's house. Others are not quite so kind to me as my father and mother were.

B. You see, much remains still to be done, in order to make even England quite perfect, and all Englishmen like one family.

A. But when that is accomplished, what shall we have to do?

B. If that ever be accomplished, (and, though I discern no sign of its nearing, I would not pronounce it impossible) people will feel no want of work. They will go forth and make all the rest of the world as perfect as England.

A. And when that is done, what will remain?

B. To go to heaven.

A. It will be hardly worth while changing

our quarters, after they have become so pleasant.

B. Perhaps not. Who knows what may happen then! But at all events we shall not soon be turned on our heavenly parish for lack of employment. God, when he laid on us the command to labour, supplied us with plenty of materials: he gave us a world to people, to cultivate, and to humanize: we had to imprint man's image on the whole earth, and to renew God's image within ourselves. When all this is achieved, and nothing is left, should such a time ever arrive, we may perhaps expect that he, who in his wisdom gave the command, in the same wisdom will revoke it. u.

Man's labour is half spent in doing over a second time what was ill done at first.

Pouvoir, c'est vouloir. u.

Follies like comets have their periodical returns. *␣␣␣␣␣␣␣␣␣␣␣␣␣␣␣␣␣␣␣␣␣␣␣␣␣␣␣␣␣␣␣␣␣␣␣␣␣␣*v.

Surely men must have been Centaurs originally. At least it is on horseback they seem to enjoy the full perfection of their nature: so that the argument by which Aristophanes in Plato's *Banquet* demonstrates the primeval existence of Androgynes, is equally cogent here. *␣␣␣␣*v.

Barrow, in a letter to Skinner about the treatise *de Doctrina Christiana*, warns him against having any concern with *one Milton*. This was several years after the publication of *Paradise Lost*. He who calls to mind how eminent a man Barrow himself was, may learn hence rightly to estimate the worth of contemporary reputation. *␣␣␣␣␣␣␣␣*v.

No two pairs of eyes see the same thing in the same thing. U.

What do people mean by being jealous of one another's fame? Are they afraid of such a run upon Glory, as may bankrupt her before they can get their due? Sooner will two rogues have to fight for the last halter in the world, than two great men for the last crown of glory. Sooner will the stars jostle against each other in the sky, than any shall be wronged for want of room in Glory's illimitable firmament. Glory is not a mistress or wife, that her affections should be monopolized: her love is as a mother's love, which spreads equally over all her children, and seems almost to grow in capacity and intensity, as if her heart expanded, with the increase of her family. Do we wish to be received into that family? let us begin by treating all its members as our elder brethren. Man's powers of admiration, like all his spiritual faculties, in proportion as they are congenial to his nature, are enlarged and strengthened by exercise. Let us then exercise them constantly, by helping him to discern whatever is admirable in others: so may we hope that, as he becomes familiar with the aspect of excellence, he will the more readily recognize it, if there be anything excellent in us. U.

Many persons seem to keep their hearts in their eyes: you come into both together, and so you go out of them. Others are wonderfully fond of you, when at a distance, but grow cold on your entering the house; as if the meaning of representing Love blind, were, that he cannot see and love. With the former the imagination is a mere footman to walk behind the senses and hold up their train; in the latter the imagination has quarrelled with the senses, never alert save when they are sleeping, sulky and speechless the instant they awake. The imagination I say; because the activity of the imagination is indispensable to all affection. It is not the bare object, as it strikes our vision at the moment, that is the object of affection: it is that object arrayed in all the attributes wherewith the imagination invests it, in part from recollection, in part creatively by inference; or rather it is the person to whom the imagination, the only personifying faculty, the faculty which combines qualities into character, assigns all those amiable attributes. Fortunate then and precious are those hearts in which the imagination and the senses move in harmonious unison with each other and with the affections, which care not about the accidents of time and space, the love of which can neither be undermined by absence, nor overturned or shaken by presence. υ.

No book has ever been read and interpreted in so many different ways as the book of life: and no wonder, seeing that all other books are only transcripts from some part of it. It contains not a line, but one man will tell you it is straight, another crooked, a third forked, a fourth curved, a fifth zigzagged. It contains not a passage, but one man sees mischief crouching at the end of it, while his neighbour perceives joy there echoing back his smiles. Every volume is like the Herculanian: if you touch it rashly and presumptuously, it crumbles: but unfold it with care and reverence, you find it inscribed with the characters of wisdom.

What can be the origin of these differences? Is life, as God's gift, multiform, and the mind which receives and contemplates it, simple and single? or is life one and the same, while it is the mind of man that " makes a heaven of hell, a hell of heaven?" The question is akin to that which has been so vehemently agitated about the nature of light, whether the ray is complex, every coloured object imbibing only a portion of it, or whether the ray is simple, and the differences of colour arise from differences in the object illumined. On a matter so much disputed among far abler judges, I presume not to do more than guess that, whatever may be the true solution in the one case, the true solution in the other will be similar. The analogy between light and life almost convinces me that it must be so. u.

It is curious to observe how some men's thoughts gravitate upward, some downward. Brutes can apprehend and have the affections of humanity: why should brutes be less than men? Beasts can apprehend and have the affections of humanity: why should men be more than beasts?

The history of philosophy is the history of a game at cat's cradle. One theory is taken off; and then the taker off holds out a second to you, of the same thread, and very like the first, although not quite the same. According to the skill of the players, the game lasts through more or fewer changes: but mostly the string at length gets entangled, and you must begin afresh, or give over; or at best the cat's cradle comes back again, and you have never a cat to put into it.   U.

Truth, they say, lies at the bottom of a well; and few, I suppose, have not once in their life sighed: *If I could but get her out of it!* Now the greater part of the world never make out which is the well: they think it must be some very marvellous fine one, a long long way off: their own, they are sure, contains nothing of the sort. Very many look down into it, and see nothing, and pass on. A good number begin to draw her up; but after a turn or two find it hard work, and stop. A smaller number, more determined, pull rather longer; till growing faint they wish to ascertain their progress, and beholding a dazzling light are frightened, think the earth must be on fire, and run away: it being a well, they had inferred that Truth must be a kind of water, and fancied she would be the very thing for their flower-pots, or for their plants. Some hold out till they get a sight of her features; when finding little likeness to what their glass had assured them the face ought to be, they make no doubt of Truth being an impostor, and tumble her down again. A very few have brought her up near the ground: but having her there they begin to parley, and bargain that she shall say just what they bid her; and on her laughing and exclaiming *Oh no! that's impossible!* they call her a pert ungrateful slut, who, for all they care, may roll back to the bottom and be drowned.

In short, people seem to be nearly all of one mind, that where Truth has lain since the beginning of the world, she may continue to lie till the end of it. If she is at all nearer the top now than she was four thousand years ago, it is chiefly by reason of the rubbish which has fallen into the well and choked up the bottom.

As for going down the well, I never heard of any except Aristotle who tried it: he did it, they tell you, to look at a star: perhaps he had other purposes also; and who knows how many of his works he found there! u.

A philosopher is Truth's minister: he usually fancies himself her favorite, forgetting that she has none, or thinking that she must make an exception in his behalf. u.

One of the greatest benefits which a wise man in these days could bestow on mankind, would be by inventing a safety-lamp to work the mines of Truth with. But have we not already got one? I dare say we have; and it only needs to be discovered and applied. υ.

―――

Does anybody really believe that the sun is as big as the little plot of ground he is standing on?
υ.

―――

The worst person one can think about, is oneself. υ.

―――

Men harm others by their deeds, themselves by their thoughts. υ.

―――

How often one sees people looking far and wide for what they are holding in their hands! Why! I am doing it myself at this very moment. υ.

Truth is our intellectual Canaan. The children of this world are only to be enticed thither by the fruit of it, the grapes, pomegranates, and figs; yet even these baits cannot overcome their dread of the giants, the children of Anak, whom they suppose to dwell there. The wise man ascends the steep mountain, and views the promised land, and when he has fully seen it, his body can no longer hold his spirit, and he passes into it, as Moses did, through death.　u.

We scoff at the men of old as gross and sensual and carnal-minded, because they were for ever seeing the devil. Is it quite certain that we do not manifest a mind yet coarser, a spirit yet more beset and besotted by sense, in never seeing him? One may grow so familiar with one's chains, as to forget that one wears them; nor is insensibility to dirt an infallible criterion of cleanliness. At all events the devil has enough of the fox in him to keep out of sight, unless we unearth him. υ.

Some people are content to be ignorant of what they do not know; others are not. The former may be called negative ignorance, the latter positive. The first is commonest among the men who know the most, the other among those who know the least. It may be recognized at once like a horse's age by the mouth: for it is always big-mouthed and foul-mouthed. It immediately concludes that what it knows not, is not worth knowing; and hastens to tell the world so, and that this is the reason of its having neglected the study. Thus for instance, the abuse squirted upon the middle ages has mostly come from those who were strangers to them, or at least from those who could not comprehend them: for, as everybody is aware, the difference is important between the entrance of an object into the mind, and the entrance of the mind into the object.　　　U.

When any one declaims against the schoolmen, I would hold up the *Summa Theologiæ* of St. Thomas Aquinas, and desire him to read and to understand it, before he presumed to assert that there is nothing in the schoolmen. This argument would knock him down as effectually, as Johnson's folio knocked down the poor bookseller.　　　　　　　　　　　　　　　　J. U.

The Greeks and Romans were citizens; the English, French, Germans, Spaniards, Italians, are subjects: and no enterprise in the history of the world, since that which was confounded on the plain of Shinar, has been so signally discomfited, as the attempt to introduce citizenship amongst us. The ancients perhaps, at least the Spartans and the Romans, drew too tight the bonds which attached the man to the state, and thereby at once thwarted his growth and cramped the freedom of his action. Much to be sure was gained by this: but the damage was not less. Sparta was full of great Spartans; Rome was full of great Romans; and yet there was hardly ever a great man either at Sparta or at Rome. For a great man is a man of God's making, not of man's making; if man meddles too much with it, he is sure to mar his maker's work: he should be content to bring out the original colours, by cleaning the picture and by varnishing it; and even this ought to be done cautiously and charily. Whereas the Romans had too many marks of human workmanship about them. They stood like yews in a clipt hedge, forming indeed a solid impenetrable mass, admirable above all things for defence, deadening whatever lay beneath them: but you could not disengage one tree or distinguish it from its neighbours; hardly could you tell where the first ended and the next began. The ploughshare of civil institutions had been driven once and again over the whole nation; and its aspect was as monotonous and featureless as the surface of a furrowed field. You pass through their history as along their roads, in one straight uniform never-ending dreary despotical line: start where you will, advance far as you will, the same boundless length of trodden barren road still presses upon your eyes, and almost pierces them. In truth I know nothing more wearisome than a Roman road: *Propria quæ maribus* is lively to it: if it saves you, as they say, a few minutes by the clock, it doubles the time by the dial within the breast. I have never landed at Dover, without recurring in thought during the first stage to those fine lines of Schiller:

> The road of Order, even though it bend,
> Is never devious. Straight on goes the lightning;

Straight is the cannon-ball's terrific path;
Rapidly, by the nearest way, it comes,
And shattering rushes onward, still to shatter.
My son, the road which human beings travel,
Along which Blessing journeys, ever follows
The river's turns, the valley's playful windings,
Curves round the cornfield and the hill of vines,
Honouring the holy bounds of property.

My version of this passage from the *Wallenstein* (Act I. Sc. IV.) has been helped out by an imperfect recollection of Coleridge's excellent translation, which, like many of the best books published a quarter of a century ago, is become a great rarity. The last two lines belong entirely to him; and I have retained his epithet *holy*, as better suited to my purpose than Schiller's expression, *the measured bounds of property*. Yet this change in its original place, where the words come from Octavio Piccolomini, is clearly injurious. No man knows better than Mr. Coleridge that what may be ideally the best, may not be dramatically or characteristically the fittest;

a distinction however which only few poets have duly perceived, and very few have not frequently lost sight of: for the observance of it requires an imagination that never slumbers. A meditative man, accustomed to contemplate God's workings in man's doings, may discern a holiness in the institutions of property: even the Romans in their religious age venerated Terminus as a deity. Or had the speech belonged to the younger Piccolomini, *holy* might have been appropriate: but a subtile intriguing statesman like his father would look only to the interests of this world, and behold the good of order and measure, rather than anything holy, in the strict observance of civil rights. Would that such men could always see even this!

To resume the former discussion I cannot remark the striking contrast between an English highway and a French, I cannot turn round the corner of some poor man's field, or see the road, as it does in some places, almost recoiling upon itself, without rejoicing, and blessing the country in which " the holy bounds of property" have been thus " honoured." Our modern improvements indeed are busily doing away with such idle useless incumbrances upon the public, that amorphous many-carcased idol to which the pleasure and happiness of every body are now so anxiously sacrificed: but, thank Heaven! all traces of a better time cannot be easily obliterated. We must still be the children of our ancestors, not our own: fortunate will it be for our children if they are so likewise, if the blood of their forefathers prevails in their veins over that of their fathers. For the tendency in modern Europe has on the whole been to " honour the holy bounds" of individuality, the landmarks of property in character. At least it has been so, as I noticed some time since, among the nations of the Teutonic race: and even among those whose language indicates that in the confluence of the two mighty streams the Celto-Latin was predominant, in earlier times, before the conquerors had been fused and dissipated among the conquered, and before they had learnt that they ought to be ashamed of their own features, and to paint them over, and to mimic the nature of another people instead of perfecting their own, we find abundant evidence of individuality and originality, that is, of genius, which makes us proud of belonging to the same family. When reading Montaigne or Rabelais or Cervantes or Dante, we feel more akin to them, more as if we were reading English authors, than when we look into their later countrymen: and the reason is, that in the former the human spirit is more powerful than the national, the genial than the formal: for our heart makes answer to every voice of nature, while our intellect, unwearied in devising artifices of its own, fences itself in against the intrusion of any artifices from without.

The contrast between the two characters is illustrated in its various bearings by the contrast between the armies of the two periods; between the legionary service of the Roman *miles*, whose name told him that he was only one of a thousand, and the feudal services of the knights and their retainers, every one of whom was a *man-at-arms*, surrounded by his friends and neighbours, and never passing out of his domestic circle or losing the thought and presence of his home, not even when fighting on foreign ground. " There cannot easily be any so degraded, (says the chivalrous Fouquè), that his heart does not swell within him, when in the moment of glorious danger he hears the name of his dear home. *The Brandenburgers to the charge!* cries a general galloping up; *Brandenburgers on!* cry the officers: and the town of Brandenburg and the whole beloved country rise up together in the souls of the brave soldiers, and the forms too of wife and child and mother, or of her who in hope is as a wife, of all the dearly loved gentle helpless ones, they too rise up and look at us affectionately, and intreatingly and with an eye that minds us to do our duty: of a truth one fights well then:" (*Gefühle, Bilder und Ansichten*, v. I. p. 213.) There was nothing like this in the Roman armies, that is, in the later times of the republic: the expedition of the Fabii belongs to its chivalrous age, and seems to imply that much then was otherwise. But the Roman people, such as we best know it, might have answered with the demoniac, that its name was Legion. It was possessed by one spirit, a spirit made up of the spirits of all the Romans: and no man could bind it, no, not with chains; neither could any man tame it. At last however, when it saw Jesus in the glory of his doctrine, the holders of the spirit were become as a herd of swine, and the herd ran violently down into the sea of destruction, and were choked in the sea of destruction.

In modern times on the contrary the great difficulty has been to infuse any thing like a national consciousness into the people, to induce the individual to consider himself as a member of the body politic, as an integral part of the one great integral whole. Many persons, I am afraid, have never found out that there were any bonds connecting them with the state, until they made the discovery in a prison. Now although the architecture of a state should, I think, be of that kind which is called Cyclopian, in which the large blocks are craftily and mightily made fast, without being squared and shaven of all their knobs and ruggednesses, as the Romans squared and shaved them for their wall, where every stone was a mere facsimily of its neighbour; still they ought to be combined in some way; they ought to strengthen and comfort each other: whereas too often in modern history all the great stones are seen to lie scattered about the ground, the walls, such as they are, being made up of pebbles and rubbish.

If we wish to know the prime reason of all this, we must trace it up, as we must trace up whatever is most extensively and permanently influential over human nature, to religion; in its action, or in its inertness. The only thing which can uphold man against the world, which can preserve his principles from growing tortuous and his genius from being benumbed, is religion. But the religion of the Romans was too weak to contend with the power of the state. Rome was a greater deity than any that inhabited the heavens. So long as they wrought together, all went well, at least in outward seeming. But when the earthly god deposed the heavenly, it signed the forfeiture of its own franchise; it became a mere nothing and fell to the ground. There was no vital indestructible essence in heathenism, to enable it, as Christianity has so often, to revive in the very season of its greatest oppression, and to shoot out most healthily and vigorously, just after the world fancied it had cut it down. Thus the religious consciousness of the Romans was weak, when at variance with their political consciousness. Christianity has reversed this: it has set up the spiritual law of God in all its simplicity and purity high above the complicated machinery of human legislation: we are not merely to do what man commands; we are to look into our own hearts; we are to commune with them; we are to bring them into accordance with the Bible and into communion with God. In this way men have naturally been led to a stronger discernment of their own individuality, and a more scrupulous developement of the gifts which God has given them, without reference to their political value. But that such contemplations, unless they be followed with the utmost meekness and humility, may easily mislead those who pursue them, to form very irregular notions of their civil duties, is apparent; even without the evidence to be derived from the conduct of the Anabaptists, of our own fifth-monarchy men, and of other religious fanatics. Still, as in the days of Christ, one of the hardest things for men to persuade themselves of, is, that the Kingdom of Heaven is not the Kingdom of Earth. υ.

I knew a man who went to church once a year, on the Martyrdom of Charles. υ.

Heliogabalus is said to have calculated the size of Rome from ten thousand pounds weight of cobwebs amassed within it. Mr. Colquhoun and the Reports of the Police and Mendicity Committees have furnished us with similar materials for estimating the grandeur of our own metropolis. Only the dirt is moral. u.

Good criticism is nice. u.

Positive Law is the shield behind which we are to wage battle in the cause of Duty. If our souls were of adamant and invulnerable by the powers of Evil, we should not need it. And our instructions are like the charge of the Spartan mother, ἢ τὰν, ἢ ἐπὶ τάν. The fate of Sandt at once illustrates and confirms this. u.

Life is the hyphen between matter and spirit.
u.

L' Homme a le droit de raisonner, et la liberté de deraisonner. Mais il tient à ses libertés, plus qu'à ses droits. L'une est privilege, l'autre est devoir. υ.

C'est bien vrai : Platon est visionnaire, car il voit. υ.

Veritatis zonam nulla solvit manus nisi Amoris. υ.

What is possible? What you will. υ.

"A man's errors are what renders him amiable," says Goethe in the last number of his *Journal on Art*, that is, in his seventy-seventh year.

I said one day to a girl of fourteen: *If you were but as good as your brother!*

Well! she replied, with something of a bashful sullenness. *I don't care. You would not be so fond of me, if I was.*

This coincidence between the aged poet and the child just emerging from childhood—laugh not, reader! Goethe himself would be delighted to be told of it—might suggest many reflexions on the waywardness of the heart and the perverse nature of affection. But I will not pursue them, having only brought these sayings together, that they may explain and support a remark in the other volume. (p. 211—214.)   U.

L'amour est un bien, ou un bonbon.   U.

People can seldom brook contradiction, except within themselves.   U.

Some thoughts are acorns. Would that any in this book were!   U.

A child must be borne long, before he is born.   U.

Suspect the wisdom which is always blaming.
    R.

"The crown of martyrdom" is the only honour which men are fonder of bestowing than receiving. R.

When a gainful wrong is to be done, a man's charity forbids his leaving it as a qualm for the conscience of his neighbour. R.

Is it truth or satire, that nothing is condign but punishment? U.

On veut toujours être quelque chose : c'est dommage qu'on n'y reussit point. On ne veut pas être soi-même ; on y reussit. La personnalité ne s'acheve que par nous-mêmes ; mais nous ne pouvons nous en debarrasser. U.

The sorriest proof of your being in the Faith, is, asserting that your brother is out of it. Many Roman-catholics call Protestants heretics ; many

Protestants call Roman-catholics heathens. God grant both may be wrong! U.

After wading through a treatise to prove that man is only an animal in whom selfishness has put on a mask, how heartening it is to read the second commandment, and to find that the motive, by which, as being the most powerful, we are deterred from idolatry, is the love of our children. U.

I love to gaze on a breaking wave. It is the only thing in nature which is most beautiful in the moment of its dissolution. U.

Coleridge ought to have written a poem on the falls of Schaffhausen, as a companion for his hymn on Mont Blanc. To me that fall was certainly the most majestic sight I had yet seen; and so awakening were the images and emotions it called up, that I could not refrain from attempting to embody them in words, at the very moment when I was possest with the fullest consciousness that no words could represent to myself, much less convey to others, the rushings and whirls and flashes and roar, the mountains of foam and columns of spray, which had just been surrounding and amazing me. We are too lavish of strong expressions in speaking of little things, to have a sufficient store of them in reserve for great. What is louder than thunder? what more momentary in brightness, more awful in rapidity, than lightning? And yet these two superlatives of nature are called in day after day, to give consequence to cracks and sparkles, until we reach this mighty waterfall without an image or allusion left to impart a notion of what the eye and ear are feeling.

The Rhine at Schaffhausen is already a considerable stream, some hundred feet in breadth.

Between the town and the fall, which is about half a league from it, the river, after making two right angles in its course, turns abruptly and makes yet another, to plunge headlong down a precipice of seventy or eighty feet. We crossed it at Schaffhausen, and followed the left bank through vineyards, until the walls of Laufen Castle, which overhangs the fall, prevented our proceeding further. We then mounted the rock on which the castle stands, and while waiting for the key of the door that was to admit us to a sight of the cataract, I looked out of a window in the court, and saw the Rhine already emerged from the fall, but still one stream of foam, flowing on and gradually changing colour, until it disappeared betwixt two quiet banks of green, itself also by that time as green and quiet as if it had never been disturbed. The door was now unlocked, and we descended a steep winding path, until we found ourselves in a little jutting gallery, opposite to the cascade, and within its spray. Then opened on my eyes and ears (which hitherto I had deafened purposely, to avoid getting accustomed to the roar of the fall, before I saw it) a scene wherein sensation for a while absorbed me. When at last I became collected enough to distinguish the sounds and sights which had astounded me, I perceived that on my left hand, very near as it then seemed to the right bank, two rocks broke the stream. Of these, one stood perhaps thirty yards before the other, and the torrent rushed furiously through the opening between them. On the left bank, just above the fall, the waters had scooped out a large basin, the issue from which into a narrow channel produced on that side of me the same violent cross-current, as the passage betwixt the two rocks produced on the other. Between these two cross-currents the main body of water fell, or rather, to speak as it looked, turned on its axis. For as the bottom of the descending stream was lost in its own vapour, this part of the river, from incessantly rolling down an unbroken mass of foam, seemed an ever-revolving avalanche crested with snowy spray. But how give an idea of the depth of sound, when the two cross streams, which had been prancing along sideways, arching their necks like warhorses that hear the trumpet, broke upon the main stream and forced their way into it! From the valley of thunder where they encountered, rose a towering misty column, behind which the river unites unseen, as though unwilling that any should witness the awfully tender reconcilement of its waters. In returning up the path, contrasting in my mind the confusion I had just left, with the comparative tranquillity of the stream above, and its subsequent beautifully gentle stillness as it winds between its green banks, I found it remind me of the one day of terror which is to separate time from eternity. The idea was strengthened, when looking back on the scene of turbulence from a summer-house immediately over it, I saw the glorious sun, that visible eye of God, not only smiling on the river in both its states of quietness, but beautifying the very fall itself with the colours of a perfect rainbow, thus brightening the depth of the extremest uproar with a gleam of light and peace, and a sign of hope.

After fully examining this side of the waterfall, we got into a boat to cross over. In our passage I discovered that what I had taken for nearly the whole stream, was little more than a third of it, and that between the right bank and the two rocks before spoken of, was a third, which divided the remainder of the river into two unequal parts, so as to make three cascades in all. One has been already described. The middle fall is perhaps the broadest, and, though not so interesting as either of its brethren, brings its waters down with great dignity in one straight unbroken flood. The fall adjoining the right bank is the smallest. To this we approached very near by means of a mill which is built close to it. Here I perceived to my great delight that what previously and at a distance seemed a savage contest between the currents, is only a fiercer joyousness and the fury of mimic war. The waters, after rushing to the onset, leap back from it with a laughing exultation and boyish alacrity incompatible with hostility or hatred. The third fall is very beautiful indeed, the whole stream on that side running aslant over a bed of rocks till it tumbles forward in vast masses like enormous blocks of crystal, with edges so white and brilliant, so sudden in appearance, and following one another, with a speed so glancing, that they gave me the idea of frost lightnings.

On my return home, overflowing with admiration of the Rhinefall, I was told that I must be mistaken, for that most English travellers are disappointed by it. Perhaps this is owing to people's fondness for reading detailed accounts of the spots they are to visit, thus learning to look through other eyes instead of with their own; especially as most descriptions mean to embellish or magnify, and if a man sees a serpent a hundred feet long, the odds are he will tell you it was a hundred and fifty. Else tourists form in their own minds notional conceptions of what this and that object must be; and then, because Nature's Rhinefall is not a copy of their's, they blame her for differing from their pattern, forgetting that her's was made first:

" For when we are there, although 'tis fair,
  It is another Yarrow."

All these things, and the flutter incident to expectation, render the mind unapt for receiving that new, vigorous, and exact impression, which alone is beautiful or lasting. Surely, the best way of taking the bent of a thing, is, to yield to its sway and there fix. But should not the imagination in studying poetry—and a tour in Switzerland is nothing else—be active? Yes; when it has first been passive. To do anything worth doing, we must have suffered. The quality most fatal to a general, says Napoleon somewhere in his Memoirs, is a propensity " de se faire des tableaux." It is to this propensity, equally destructive of knowledge and of taste, that I would attribute the disappointment of my countrymen at Schaffhausen.

Widely different from this picture-making are the modest anticipations of the true poet. He too perhaps dreams of rock and wood and yawning depths, and the restless might of an imprisoned river, or, it may be, of noble waters struggling for precedency down the rush of danger; but all this while he knows himself to be dreaming, and knows moreover that he can only dream a dream. Truth, the presence of the desired object arouse him: he opens his senses and mind wide to the spectacles which nature has prepared, and submits his visions dutifully to her realities. His perceptions of beauty are too quick not to discover in a thousand points the justness and harmony of her workings; and his imagination, flexible as well from practice as from inherent powers of modulation, readily takes its tone from hers. Not even in those extreme cases where the anticipation had been so long fostered in the fancy as to have taken root, is the reality excluded by it from the poet's mind: his spirit is large enough for both; and they flourish together in it like two brotherly trees that unite to make one great tree between them. But why say in prose, what has been already said much better in verse? Wordsworth, who in 1803, sang of *Yarrow Unvisited*, eleven years afterward sang thus of Yarrow visited:

> " But thou, that didst appear so fair
>   To fond imagination,
>   Dost rival in the light of day
>   Her delicate creation.
>   *   *   *   *
>   I see; but not by sight alone,
>   Fair region, have I won thee;
>   A ray of fancy still survives,
>   Her sunshine plays upon thee.
>   *   *   *   *
>   And yet I know, where'er I go,
>   Thy *genuine* image Yarrow,
>   Will dwell with me, to highten joy,
>   And cheer my mind in sorrow.

To translate La Fontaine's fables is as idle, as to decant a bottle of Champagne: the spirit evaporates; and there is not much else... U.

Hardly any odour is so noisome as that of a perfumer's shop; if some friend would but hint this to the author of *Lalla Rookh*. I have known that poem give a head-ache, just like the *Passage Feydeau*. u.

———

One often hears of characters being *whitewashed*. *Yellow-washed* would be an apter expression: for in such cases gold has about twenty times the potency of silver. Indeed the Stock-Exchange would lead one to suspect that the yellow fever must be the healthiest state of man. All are so eager to catch it. u.

———

Few are very ready to give, except to those who want nothing. They conceive, I fancy, that they are fulfilling the promise: *unto every one that hath shall be given.* That the second part of the same promise should never fail, has been the prime care of all the governments which have ever existed. u.

———

Never tell a person, you mean no offence. If you really mean to give none, it is an insult to suppose he will take it. Much oftener however your very defence implies the consciousness of having offended. People seldom wrap a rag round a finger which has nothing the matter with it. But hollow things sound readily.

u.

———

I believe the correct definition of a busybody to be: a person who has nothing to do, and who therefore does nothings. It is natural that such characters should be so common among old maids; where they find not a kindlier vent for their activity and for the great female instinct of busying themselves for others, in educating the children of their relations or friends, or in the superintendence and management of charitable works. u.

Some minds cannot boil, without boiling over. Let Coleridge devise any vessel for his thoughts, however eccentric its shape, however manifold its convolutions, still it will not hold them. He seldom says enough on any subject, because he always says more than enough. His works are like a forest: you are for ever losing the main road, from the number of stately allies beneath which you must pause and contemplate, the number of pleasant by-paths which lure you along them, the number of wild dingles which you cannot choose but explore. u.

Second thoughts are best, says every second person you meet; fitly enough; for second thoughts are always second-rate ones. A second thought is only a half-thought; or, according to Hamlet's more correct analysis,

> The craven scruple
> Of thinking too precisely on the event,
> A thought which quartered hath but one part wisdom,
> And ever three parts coward.

No second thought ever led a man to do anything generous, anything kind, anything great, anything good. By its very nature it can suggest nothing; except difficulties and hinderances. It objects, it demurs, it pares off, it cuts down. *I must not do this: who knows what may be the consequence? I must not engage in that: it is impossible to see the end of it. I must not go this way: there may be a precipice across it: nor that way: there may be a puddle, and I may wet my feet; and people have died of wet feet; or there may be a pebble, and it may get into my shoe, and men have been lamed for life by pebbles in their shoes. What will A say? what will B think? how will C look? will not D laugh at me?* But it is endless to enumerate the doubts, the cavils, and the quiddities, the *ifs,* the *should's,* and the *may's,* the marks of interrogation, and the marks of admiration, wherewith that father of all pettifoggers, Nothingness, barricades himself against the assaults of Enterprise.

Second thoughts, I have said, are only fragments of thoughts; that is, they are thought by a mere fragment of the mind, by a single faculty; the prudential understanding; which, though highly useful as a servant, is too fond of putting on its master's clothes, in spite of its mean carriage when wearing them. Now man, as I have before remarked of his actions, that is, of his outward thoughts, so also in his thoughts, which are his inward actions, should studiously preserve the unity of his being: his every motion, whether spiritual or corporeal, whether simple or complex, should be single as the flight of an arrow: it should be like the motion of that cloud so majestically described by Wordsworth,

> Which heareth not the loud winds when they call,
> Or moveth altogether, if it move at all.

For this is the only way to preserve its consistency and integrity: if any portion of it strays from the main body, the Cossack winds are ready to disperse it, even as the Cossacks with their windlike fleetness destroyed every straggler from the great army of Napoleon. Our first thoughts, as was observed before, though in a somewhat different point of view, (Vol. I. p. 143.) are much likelier to be just: for they are the expression of our whole being; or at least, if the feelings have a somewhat undue predominance, they still act in unison with the intellect; and moreover they have been fashioned by the intellect, and trained by the experience of our whole lives, until they have acquired that kind of discrimination which is called *tact*, from its approach to the certainty imparted by the least fallible of the senses. But when the understanding lifts up its head, grumbling because it has not been appealed to, and mutters, *this must not, may not, cannot, should not be*, the mind is no longer at one, but at six and seven; it grows as it were drunk with prudence and sees double, and falters, totters, reels, tumbles, and falls asleep.

Are we then always to halt at our first thoughts? Yes: if we cannot go beyond our second thoughts. These are only good as a half-way house to bait at in the progress to our third thoughts; which in consonance with a foregoing remark are mostly found to chime with the first, like the third line in the *Divina Commedia*, that magnificent spiritualization of all sensuous things, the very title of which declares the harmony between earth and heaven. For while great practical minds anticipate their second thoughts in their first, great speculative minds take up their first and second thoughts and reconcile them in their third. The horses of the former are harnessed as before a Grecian chariot, all four abreast, and they advance vehemently and impetuously, though not without some peril. Second-thoughted men take off their feelings, that is, their two outside horses, for fear of their kicking and plunging, and are content to plod along at a foot's pace with the heavy wheelers of the understanding. The third-thoughted man resumes his feelings, and places them as leaders in front, where they are more manageable and less likely to run foul.   u.

No earthly light is without smoke; no earthly fire but leaves embers: so is it with human virtues. Only good men have fumivores, to keep their smoke from annoying their neighbours, nay, sometimes even to fuel their flame with it: they gather up the cinders, and throw them into the fire, which never burns so clearly and steadily and quietly and durably, as after this has been done. Such is one of the many precious lessons we learn from that peerless book St. Augustin's *Confessions*. U.

The crab is among the very few native English fruit-trees. I hope the qualities it has given name to, are not likewise natives of this island. And yet one may suspect it, one may even suspect we are vain of them, from the outcry English travellers set up against the French, for not being equally ill-favoured. We are fond of bragging that they have no *comfort* in their language or in their country: they, I believe, might reply that they have no *ill-nature* in either. If so, not having the latter is a greater bliss than having the former. Nay, the former in its modern sense has a tendency to produce the latter: at least the chief effect of what we call comforts, that I know of, is, teaching people how to be, and how to make all around them, uncomfortable. So strangely do words change their meaning: a nervous arm, as Coleridge has noticed, used to be vigorous; it is grown feeble and imbecile. Comfort used to strengthen and uphold: it now relaxes and weakens and lays us prostrate on a sofa. u.

The only place where one rarely sees anybody acting a part, is on the stage. The practice there is to play double or quits, and either to act an actor, or to act oneself. u.

We are, the better sort of us, all Adams. We all have love begotten for us, not of the flesh but of the soul, sent to us we guess not whence, leading us we see not whither, garrisoning our vacant hearts against the assaults of approaching manhood, with admiration, self-forgetfulness, devotion, purity, in a word with all true nobleness, and whispering to us its own eternity if we are faithful to it and to ourselves. But the fruit is fair to look upon, and the serpent suggests that it will be pleasant to the taste, and from impatience and curiosity we eat thereof, and love becomes mortal.

Faultiness or pravity and perishableness are correlatives. The last enemy therefore must needs be Death; and he, when all others are destroyed, will fall without a struggle.

All the elements minister to man, even in their simplest unorganized state. The Earth is his abiding-place; Water supplies him with drink;

he breathes Air; and such is the beneficence of Fire, that the ancients represented it as the greatest of the goods bestowed on men by their greatest benefactor, by that intelligence which enables them to look before and after, that Prometheus who at once

Τυφλὰς ἐν αὐτοῖς ἐλπίδας κατῴκισεν,
Μνήμην θ' ἁπάντων μουσομήτορ' ἐργάτιν.

So manifold indeed is its utility, that hardly anything material can vie with it, even if it were not the chariot in which the spirits of the martyrs had mounted into heaven. u.

The impression left on the mind by the contemplation of some heroic deed, is not unlike that image of light which abides for some time on the eye after looking at the sun. And, alas! it too seldom does more than dazzle and vanish. u.

We are most of us Absaloms, caught and inextricably entangled by the beautiful locks which are our pride: and when so entrapt we fall an unresisting prey to the enemy. u.

The bitterness of heaven is sweet: how sweet then its sweetness! The sweetness of hell is bitter: how bitter then its bitterness!

Whence arises the pleasure, the eagerness, wherewith men, and women too, unless their natural appetites have been checked and refined into a nicer delicacy, if not into a fastidious daintiness, flock to the aspect of danger? What collects such a concourse around a scaffold? surely it is not a mob of vultures gathering about the carcase. What renders a ship in a storm one of the most interesting and sublimest and most fascinating spectacles? Surely it is not, as the Epicureans assert, " quibus ipse malis careas, quia cernere suave est," or, as Hobbes expresses it, because " there is Novelty and Remembrance of our own security present," *(Humane Nature, Chap. IX. 19.)* The pleasure comes rather from the arousal of the imagination, from the impetuous rush of the feelings, which ever swarm like bees at the sound of the alarm-bell, and of which the intensest and most fervid activity is always the most delightful. There is a solemn assemblage of emotions, breathless and leaning forward to listen like a devout congregation to the eloquent voice of the preacher; there is an awfulness in the turmoil of the elements upheaving wave after wave as it were sword after sword, and firing blast upon blast, to destroy their victim; it is at once fearful and joyous to behold man battling with powers to which his own, materially considered, are nowise comparable, and holding out against them, if not vanquishing and subduing them, by the courage and wisdom of his soul: we sympathize with the conflict which our brother is waging; the honour of our own spiritual natures is concerned in it; and so long as the result is still uncertain, we hope and trust that man will be victorious.

In the weak indeed, where their own personal safety is at stake, and where their fears for themselves are strongly awakened, the pain of such a situation will often overbalance the pleasure; and thus a seemingly plausible pretext is afforded for the assertion of Lucretius, that danger is only pleasant to those who are out of it. But the brave and truly human heart, be it the manly or the womanly, is distressed to witness a peril in which it cannot share; it longs to be in it, either for the sake of fighting or of helping: it rises higher and higher with the emergency; and, as I have seen eyes which have seemed to be bright with excessive darkness, so may it be said of honorable danger, that the very excess of its darkness brightens it.

In the case of an execution, it is true, most of the finer excitements are wanting; and that therefore is relished only by coarser palates, by those who feel not duly the atrocity of Crime or the majesty of Law, and who are little interrupted by such appalling thoughts while they are gazing upon the struggle between Life and Death. u.

What is material is immaterial: what is immaterial is material. u.

Μὴ ποίει ἃ ποιεῖν ἡδύ, ἀλλ' ἃ πεποιηκέναι. u.

A true knight wishes only for two allies, the prayer of Earth, and the blessing of Heaven. Let him be slain: he cares not: he is sure to live. Let him be conquered: it matters not:

he is sure to triumph. For the cause of good is the cause of God.

U.

Is not the burning bush seen by Moses an exact type of the devout heart? It too burns as with fire; and it is not consumed; for the fire is the presence of God.

Hence also we learn that destruction and mortality are of the earth earthy. The heavenly fire consumes not. The rays of the sun do not burn, unless the glass they shine through is darkened.

U.

The idea of the introduction to Goethe's *Faust* is evidently taken from the introduction to the book of Job. Pope had noticed long ago, that

> Satan now is wiser than of yore,
> And tempts by making rich, not making poor.

This is the natural progress of society. The first danger is from distress, which may sometimes drive a man into crime: the second and greater is from prosperity, which helps him to slide down into sin. The former may numb the heart, until it ceases to clench its hold; the latter too often relaxes it, so that it lets virtue drop. Even this however furnishes a very inadequate notion of the temptations by which Faust is beset. The last century had taken rapid strides toward Hell. The sons of God, man's intellectual and spiritual faculties, saw the daughters of men, their animal and sensual propensities, that they were fair; and we are not yet delivered from all the foul progeny that spawned from the unnatural concubinage. This state of being is what the great poet of our times undertook to represent, in which " every imagination of the thoughts of the heart was only evil continually." The snares which Faust falls into, are within him as well as without him; his enemy is himself; and the strength of that enemy makes him the more formidable: every feeling of his heart, every talent of his mind, every aspiration of his soul, is leagued in conspiracy against him. No wonder then he falls, and that his fall from such a hight is terrible.

Many good people, I understand, are shocked by *Faust*, and cry out that it is very profane. How loudly the same good people would have cried out against many passages in the Bible, if only they had not been in the Bible! Weak eyes may be disabled for seeing by the excess of light, no less than by the absence of it. To repeat a remark which is forced upon one daily, it would be well if these exclaimers were to bear in mind, that being easily shocked is no proof of standing fast. U.

" Toleration (says Landor) is an odious word." (*Imag. Conv.* Vol. I. p. 318.) Perhaps it is so; and yet the intolerance of men has made it the name of a virtue, nay even of a very rare one. Many may boast of it: few truly possess it, or practise it, except toward themselves. u.

The most heinous kind of blasphemy is persecution. u.

Drunkenness is usually followed by sickness: so is spiritual intoxication by spiritual depression. u.

Society every now and then wants a little bloodletting: this may be the use of wars. u.

Pour s'elever, il faut se lever. u.

Peutêtre, c'est le mot de celui qui ne peut faire. Napoleon ne s'en servoit pas. u.

Forte ne agas, at fortiter: fortibus nihil est fortuitum. u.

Rivalry among men usually begets aversion, if not hatred. We forget that we cannot press down our competitor, without sinking ourselves. We forget that every moment employed in attacking him, is so much lost from the pursuit of the prize. We might take a lesson from a racecourse: if the horses run against each other, they are likely to bolt. The sound of feet, whether behind or beside or before them, only redoubles their efforts to reach the goal. Nay, the very word *rivalry* might teach us wisdom. One cannot frame a conception of a more loving neighbourhood, than that between the opposite banks of a river, as they fix their smiling faces continually upon each other, although they vie in striving which shall convert the fertility, they both suck from the same stream, into the greatest richness and beauty. U.

What a fine vision of Honour had Aristotle

seen! when he declared, Δοκεῖ ἡ τιμὴ ἐν τοῖς τιμῶσι μᾶλλον εἶναι, ἢ ἐν τῷ τιμωμένῳ. (*Ethic.* I. 3.) Nothing can be truer: as the same thought is nobly expressed by Landor, " Glory is a light that shines from us on others, and not from others on us." (*Imag. Conv.* Vol. II. p. 585.) And surely the happiness of possessing something upon which we can look admiringly, something wherewith we can always refresh ourselves as in an Oasis, after wandering wearily through the wilderness of fallen man, something to uphold and stay our best resolves when they begin to faint and droop and hang down their heads in despondency, something whereon to pour forth all that love for our brethren which is ever rising and seeking an outlet in the generous heart, threatening, if we keep it shut up, to turn sour,—this happiness surely is far loftier and more deeply rooted than any pleasure which grows in the rotting swamps of vanity.

VOL. II.

There is satisfaction indeed in receiving the acknowledgement that we are worthy of honour: our conscience is often fearful of even whispering its approval, until prompted by some voice from without; wherefore men, as Aristotle pursues, ἐοίκασι τὴν τιμὴν διώκειν, ἵνα πιστεύωσιν ἑαυτοὺς ἀγαθοὺς ἔιναι. Moreover it is gladdening to see homage paid to Virtue, to see her majesty recognized, and to feel that the only reason which forbids our joining the chorus of her admirers, is, that she has vouchsafed to take up her abode in us, and to make our spirit her shrine. But, woe is me! what mortal can feel this! Admiration is human: self-complacency belongs only to Deity.

Admiration ennobles and blesses those who feel it. The lover is made happier by his love, than his mistress can be. Like the song of a bird, it cheers his own heart; and any pleasure it communicates to another, is only incidental and secondary. Why are we so imperatively commanded to give glory unto God? unless that we may ourselves be made godly by our worship. Nor, if in divine things one may speak of motives, is it easy to conceive any worthier motive why God should have revealed his glory, than that man might be glorified by contemplating it. Therefore is it our bounden duty to give thanks to him for his great glory. u.

Philosophy is the love of wisdom: Christianity is the wisdom of love. u.

Vita hominis magna sit instauratio. u.

It was a strange fancy for the man who declared that admiring nothing is the only way of being happy, to take it into his head that he was born to be a poet, and of all poets a lyrical. For while other poetry is the portraiture of feeling lyrical poetry is the utterance of it: and our feelings cannot rise into the etherial regions of poetry, until they are refined and purified and borne upward by admiration. v.

It is not the subsequent seriousness that is hypocritical, but the previous air of carelessness and levity; an air not only more likely to be assumed from being less congenial to our nature, but also more capable of being put on for an occasion, as blasphemy is more easily feigned than prayer.

Many pretend to be better than they are. One can understand this: it may serve their turn in this world, although in the next it can only deepen their damnation. But society in course of time growing high, breeds a strange race of vermin, a set of people who pretend to be worse than they are, a if they were paying court to the Devil, and making interest with him against their being received into his household. Fearful is the peril of such men; incalculable is the mischief of their example: and yet there is more hope of them than of the others. u.

Fine ladies paint...just like savages. A.

One sees a number of people sunning themselves in the moonshine. u.

A person given to barefaced flattery, will usually balance the account with interest in your absence. A.

He who amuses his guests by satirizing their friends, pays a poor compliment to the understandings which selected them. A.

Unbelief is the offspring of refinement. The fool might have said in his heart *there is no God;* but even the fool would have kept it to himself, unless he had hoped to make a noise in the world by divulging it. R.

Timid persons are afraid of learning and science and knowledge, as leading to atheism, or at least to infidelity. And yet the Psalmist has pronounced that it is the fool, who says in his heart *there is no God.* This should be the text for a sermon on the divine and godly tendencies of knowledge. In these days, when many are doubting whether Truth be Truth, people need to be especially and frequently reminded of the distinction so accurately laid down by Bacon, that "a little Philosophy inclineth man's mind to Atheism, but depth in Philosophy bringeth men's minds about to Religion. For while the mind of man looketh upon second causes scattered, it may sometimes rest in them and go no further: but when it beholdeth the chain of them confederate and linked together, it must needs fly to Providence and Deity." No finer proof of this can be given, than Bacon's own *Confession of Faith*, that magnificent outpouring of the " understanding which is the knowledge of the holy." U.

When philosophers tell us there will be no time in Heaven, I conclude they mean there will be no measure of time, that is, of succession; for time essentially is nothing more. That after a happy resurrection of the body there will be no succession of sensations, that in a happy life of any kind there will be no succession of emotions, is certainly unimaginable, and, I fancy, is nowhere revealed. True, the succession of emotions may be imperceptible;

but to render it so, we must strip our eternity of reflexion.

' The eternal *now* of Hell is much more conceivable; and it strikes me as being the most terrible form under which the idea of Hell can be presented to us. To be for ever buried, or rather suspended alive, in the same dark atmosphere of pain, able to see, hear, and touch, but neither seeing nor hearing nor even touching, deprived of all capacities of action, that the whole man may be more entirely given up to suffering,—who would bear the burthen of this bodiless tomb, that could fly from it to the flames and ice of which Milton has composed his Pandemonium?

A Christian preacher ought to keep in mind that he is not a heathen philosopher, that he is not a political orator, that he is not a stage-player; the last especially, if he is called to preach in a fashionable chapel. U.

Affectation is offensive in all places: in the pulpit it is noisome. The twang of the conventicle is not the twang of Apollo's silver bow. U.

Coxcombical indolence makes many infidels: stupid indolence keeps many Christians.

Few are aware that they want any thing, except pounds shillings and pence. U.

Seeking is not always the way to find; or Altamira would have found a husband long ago. A.

It is natural that affluence should be followed by influence. U.

Henry's chief fault is having too humble an opinion of himself.

Do pray let him keep it then; if it be only as a rarity. u.

The human soul, if holiness is to abide in it, ought to grow up, like the temple of Jerusalem, in silence. The stones of which it is constructed, the materials employed to edify it, should be " made ready before they are brought thither." u.

How well it were if we knew nothing of evil, except that it is the opposite and the adversary of good! This perhaps is the definition of innocence. u.

The ultimate tendency of civilization is toward barbarism.

The spirit of colonies has in all ages had a

democratical bias. Nations seldom think of sending out colonies, until they have reached a certain pitch of civilization, and of that practical knowledge which springs from a familiarity with the forms and circumstances of civilized or congregated life. Now Despotism finds it difficult to establish its throne, except on the flats of Ignorance, even as the Pyramids arose not among the mountains of Upper, but among the sands of Lower Egypt: at least the only other soil which does not shake it off as with an earthquake, is the putrid pestilent marsh of a people in its decrepitude. Again, in a colony all institutions are modern and as it were of yesterday, so that their utility must be palpable and immediate: they cannot possess the suitableness and expediency consequent on long usage, which make the abandoning old habits and customs, even mischievous or evil ones, an affair not only of difficulty but of danger alike to nations and individuals; neither can they excite that reverential affection which twines its evergreen foliage around all things ancient, blending with and hightening their beauties, veiling their weaknesses, and concealing the footsteps of decay, which it too often hastens even by its own action, as well as by preventing timely repairs. A recently founded state has no such feelings: it is not enough there for a practice to exist: every citizen wants to know some good reason for its continuance. Besides, colonists are mostly men of ambition, always of enterprise: among them are to be found many of those whom their own restlessness or the pressure of circumstances has irritated into discontent with the government of their native land. In their new home intellect and industry must be the means of eminence; and intellect will hardly raise a man to any considerable hight above his fellows, except where an army or a mob heave him up on their shields or on their shoulders. Now a mob is the settlement to be found in none except an old state of society. Colonies too from their situation, from the purposes which dictated the choice of it, and from other causes, are generally commercial: but Commerce holds no commerce save with the free.

These remarks, it is clear, apply not to the military colonies of the Romans. They were things of a different kind, mighty engines of stifling oppression, cities of police-officers keeping watch and ward against the struggles of independence, the craftiest device of the craftiest politicians whom the world ever saw. It is not easy to estimate their importance: the laws and languages of half Europe bear witness to it: but in themselves they were little or nothing, and rather machines than beings. U.

Use begets use. U.

Professional education might entail on our posterity all the evils of Indian castes. R.

———

None ever appropriated like the Romans. They incorporated into their empire not only provinces, but gods. R.

———

Men have in all ages been readily brought to mortify their bodies much; as the penances, wearisome pilgrimages, and tortures, which fill every superstitious code, attest. But scarcely can they be induced by any means to mortify their minds a little. So much fonder is man of his soul than of his body; in other words, so much nearer is the soul to him, so much more essentially himself.

Can we then be really fond of that about which we are so negligent? How do we shew ourselves to be so? as the fondest of all fond things, a foolish mother, does, by spoiling it.

Augustus made Tiberius adopt Germanicus, " quo pluribus munimentis insisteret." (*Tacit. Ann.* I. 3.) He was too strong to be afraid of his strongest support, and too wise to distrust where security was safety. But few sovereigns have been equally politic. In Asia they seem to think that relations are only suckers which weaken the royal stem and must be cut off, and that the only use of a king's brothers is to garnish a coronation with heads. Even Tiberius, although he had among men a pre-eminence like the serpent's, that was " more subtile than any beast of the field," made haste to forget this lesson, the best thing his stepfather ever gave him. u.

Other animals war against the animals of other kinds. It is the prerogative of man to war against his own kind. Among animals too,

I believe, fratricide prevails in proportion as they become domesticated. u.

It is a most mischievous notion that allowances are to be made for lofty and powerful minds: such indulgence encourages evil, and flatters it and foments it. Let allowances be made for the weak, in proportion to their weakness: but to whom much is given, from them let much be required. u.

We are tardy in finding out the beauty of Order: our upstart will cannot be readily brought to acknowledge the sublimity of Law. On the contrary, we prate about the uncontrolable vehemence of Greatness, the excursive vagaries of Genius: as if forsooth the uniformity of the sun's march detracted from its glory, as if the orderliness of the universe, by which the Greeks were so charmed that they called the world

Κόσμος or Order, and made the endeavour to conform thereto the regulative principle of their minds, could in any wise lessen its majesty or loveliness. None but a madman would wish to turn the former into a comet, or to melt and stir up the latter in the yawning caldron of chaos.   U.

If Genius overflow, it is, like the Nile, to fertilize.   U.

Experience is the best of teachers. Doubtless: if anybody would go to her school. But hardly one person in a hundred can learn anything from the experience of others; and hardly will one in ten learn much from his own. Let a father have ruined his fortune, his health, his character, by indulgence in any bad propensity; let him have repented and reformed his life, and been diligent in warning his son against the sins of which he retains a painful consciousness, the chance is that the son will still try to pick his way through the same mire in which his parent foundered. Though we scorn the moth for returning to the flame it has just singed its wings in, the moth might with more justice scorn and jeer at the gigantic folly of the creature gifted with reason, who in defiance of exhortation, in spite of suffering, keeps fluttering about the flames of hell, until he falls into them. U.

―――

The effects of human wickedness are written on the page of history in characters of blood; but the impression soon fades away; so more blood must be shed to renew it. U.

―――

Few take advice, or physic, without wry faces at it. U.

Who is fit to govern others?

He who governs himself.

You might as well have said: nobody. U.

———

Christianity requires not only acts but dispositions, not only virtuous deeds but virtues. This is decisive of its practical disinterestedness. Selfish alms-giving is possible; but the Gospel enjoins love, and selfish love is a contradiction. Why then does it hold out punishments and rewards as motives? Among other reasons, to keep men from being over-weighted by the world, and in the first instance to induce the acts, a perseverance in which, if sanctified by prayer, at length superinduces the disposition. The motives which in childhood made us learn to read, are not the reasons why we now love reading; but it is plain that, to love reading, we must first have learnt to read. As Coleridge says philosophically: "the mind and conscience may be reconciled to such motives, in the foreknowledge of the higher principle, and with a yearning toward it that implies a foretaste of future freedom. The enfeebled convalescent is reconciled to his crutches, and thankfully makes use of them; not only because they are necessary for his immediate support, but likewise because they are the means and conditions of exercise, and 'by exercise of establishing *gradatim paullatim* that strength, flexibility, and almost spontaneous obedience of the muscles, which the idea and cheering presentiment of health hold out to him. He finds their value in their present necessity, and their worth as they are the instruments of finally superseding it." *Aids to Reflexion*, p. 23.

And after all the being directly influenced by what the Bible has promised and denounced, is in itself wise and good. It is not only a higher and wiser, a more patient and liberal and far-minded interestedness, than any other the world can shew, (though even as such it appertains to the perfection of our prudential nature); but it must also have been preceded by a pure act of Christian virtue: for it is a preference of faith to sight, a practical acknowledgement of God in his characters of lawgiver and judge, and a manly humble seeking him as such in spite of contumely and temptation.

Like Ixion, we often embrace a cloud, and can only be awakened from our trance by a thunderbolt exploding in our arms.   U.

In the moment of our creation we receive the stamp of our individuality; and much of life is spent in rubbing off or defacing the impression.   U.

There is only one tempter whom we are very studious to withstand .. God.   U.

On doit bien aimer de perdre: on passe la vie à la perdre, et à se perdre soi-même; et il y a peu de jours où on ne fait mille choses à pure perte. U.

Why do critics make such an outcry against tragicomedies? is not life one? U.

I have been told that Lord Byron is quite as great a poet as Shakspeare, bating his universality. So Buonaparte in St. Helena was quite as powerful as Buonaparte at Paris, bating the empire of the world. U.

Jeremy Taylor's gleaming fancy plays over his deep reasoning, like the sunbeams on the sea, converting it into a flood of light. U.

The tree of knowledge is the tree of the knowledge of evil, no less than of the knowledge of good. Now if we were always certain which we got hold of, if we always knew good to be good, and evil to be evil, things might go on better. But their outward appearance is often such as to beguile those who are so ready to be beguiled; and there never is wanting a troop of conjurors and jugglers who play tricks with them, and offering us the one put the other into our hands, sophists, as the prophet denounces them, "wise in their own eyes and prudent in their own sight, calling evil good, and good evil, putting light for darkness, and darkness for light, putting bitter for sweet, and sweet for bitter." As society thickens and knowledge spreads, these blind guides multiply a hundred-fold: for while great men come forth almost like lions, singly from the womb of Time, the meanest and most noxious creatures will often have plentiful broods. Hence, while at an earlier stage great authors have to deal chiefly with men as men, with their passions and feelings, at a later they must deal with them in great measure as readers and writers, or at least with their opinions and principles. Those familiar with Goethe, and able to compare his works with Shakspeare's, will easily perceive this distinction; and when a person complains that Goethe's views of life and manners, his way of treating and representing things, are not the same with Shakspeare's, he only shews that he understands not what he is talking about. It is indeed a common practice in matters of taste, among those who have not apprehended the principles of right judgement, to judge of a thing, not by itself, but by another thing, and to condemn it because it is not something else: but this is like shooting a horse, because he has not got the horns of an ox. Goethe in 1800 does not write just as Shakspeare wrote in 1600: but neither would Shakspeare in 1800 have written just as he wrote in 1600. For the frame and aspect of society are different; the world which would act on him, and on which he would have to act, is another world. - True poetical genius lives in communion with the world, in a perpetual reciprocation of influences, imbibing feeling and knowledge, and pouring out what it has imbibed in words; of power and gladness and wisdom. It is not, at least when highest it is not, as Wordsworth describes Milton to have been, " like a star dwelling apart." Solitude may comfort weakness: it will not be the home of strength. The piety which mingles with the world and passes through it, as a great river passes through a lake, preserving the integrity of its waters, is of a far purer and mightier, as it is of a more beneficent kind, than that which shuns observation like the Niger, and goes and buries itself in a desert. Now if Religion be rather social than eremitical, surely the same holds of Genius: surely he is a greater poet who can plunge into the world, and stem its flood, and ride upon its waves, than he who loiters about the little pool of his own fancies, throwing crumbs to the gold and silver fish he has put into it. In short, Genius is not an independent and insulated, but a social and continental, or at all events a peninsular power, with a Corinthian acropolis at once connecting it with and protecting it against the main land: it must suck in its nourishment drawn from the bowels of the earth, before the strings are cut and it is launched on its voyage through time and space.

Now, without entering into a comparison of Shakspeare's age with our own, one thing at least is evident, that, considered generally and as a nation, we are more bookish than our ancestors. The mere scholar may not be so mere a scholar; but literature is more extensively diffused, and more operative on society. Our feelings come not to us directly from their objects, but through a number of mediums which have been interposed. Their wildness has been tamed; their free play has been checked; they have been taught their paces, and move in some degree according to rule: all contrasts have been softened; and we seem as it were to have passed from an uncultivated country, with its high mountains and wide dreary moors, and here and there a lovely dell lying like a smiling infant in the arms of its mailed father, into an inclosed plain, gay and prosperous and laughing, with all its fields looking one much like another. While the conflict and tug of passions supplied in Shakspeare's days the chief materials for poetry, in our days it is rather the conflict of principles: the war now is underground; the mine is dug, and we must countermine it. This appears not only from the works of Goethe and others of his countrymen, but from the course taken by our own greatest poets, by Wordsworth, Coleridge, and Landor. They have been rebuked indeed for not writing otherwise: but they have done rightly; for they have obeyed the impulse of their nature, and the voice of their age is heard speaking through their lips. In a like way our poetry has become sentimental. This too has been found fault with: but it was inevitable. A sentiment is different from a thought and from a feeling; it is a mixture of both. In its old sense it is not a mere opinion, but an opinion influencing and influenced by the character: in its modern sense, as denoting what is implied in the much abused adjective *sentimental*, a sentiment is a reflective self-conscious feeling, a feeling aware of its own existence, nursing itself, feeding itself, and too often pampering and spoiling itself.

Various considerations might arise out of the foregoing remarks: we are already in the chamber where they are sleeping; one has only to raise the coverlet, and they will jump up and beg to be dressed. Let me take the first I come to. Since knowledge, like all other earthly things, is "of a mingled yarn, good and ill together," since too at any particular time the ill is likely to be more plenteous than the good, they who enlist under the banner of literature, have a twofold duty, to extend the dominions of Truth, and to fight against and subdue the retainers of Error. Whatever may be man's chosen line of action, it lies under the operation of the original curse, and there is no doing without also undoing: not only as members of the church, but in every other capacity, while here on earth, we are militant. There are always idols which must be overthrown, and superstitions which must be rooted out; and although it may be a wholesomer and more genial employment to set up than to pull down, to produce than to destroy, still intellectual like other warfare is necessary, is unavoidable. Falsehood will lift up its impudent head, and must therefore be cast down and crushed: weeds and thorns will sprout up, and, unless they are cleared away, will choke any good seed that may be sown. But warfare, of whatever kind, is a perilous trade: even though it be undertaken in the cause of humanity, it can hardly be carried on without some inhumanity: nor is literary war less slippery than any other; nay, rather it is inwardly more dangerous, in proportion as it is less dangerous outwardly. For the immediate bodily presence of danger strengthens and elevates and therefore humanizes: but it is a fearful thing, to have the power of wounding a fellow-creature without looking him in the face, and of poisoning him with the nightshade which trickles from the pen. Nowhere is it more needful that every thing should be done calmly and temperately and deliberately, without anger or personal animosity, and with an unceasing watchfulness lest the blow fall on the offender instead of the offence. When thus waged in the spirit of love, war is not alien from poetry: for what is poetry but the language of Love? of that harmonious harmonizing spirit which looks on all things with an eye, dispassionate indeed, yet kind and complacent, not as they stand alone and may often seem to be purely mischievous, but as they spring from the abysmal sources of nature, and even when worst have still " a soul of goodness." For this reason the wisdom of the Imagination is far wiser, as it is far gentler, than the wisdom of the reflective understanding: the speculation of the latter is narrow and fragmentary and minute: but in the visions of the former all things are bathed in Love, as the stars are in the crystalline bath of the sky;

all are members of the one indissoluble universe, whereof inexhaustible Love is the radiant centre.'

What then is the proper fashion of literary warfare? The end being not personal, but the exposure and destruction of falsehood, the desirable thing must be; to apply some solvent, at the touch of which it shall crumble. Now there are two intellectual solvents: logic, which acts externally and step by step, eating away one morsel after another; and ridicule, which penetrates within, and spreads itself through every part, until by a sudden explosion it shivers the whole. In each kind the most admirable specimens are to be found among the writings of the Athenians. The demoralizing sophistry which infested and worried their republic, was assailed by the analysis of Plato and by the laugh of Aristophanes: and although they could not get rid of the disease, fomented as it was by the strongest and most irritating diet, and confirmed by the constitutional tendency of the human soul to breed in its fairest part a cancer that shall consume it, yet they must have done much good even in their own days, some nationally, more perhaps to individuals whom they startled and admonished; and their works have sounded through all after ages like warning voices of inspiration, proclaiming the dangers that encompass the unchecked aberrations of the intellect, and calling back the prodigal son to the home of his father, from feeding swine, where " he would fain have filled his belly with the husks that the swine did eat, and no man gave unto him," any more than the philosophical swineholders give nourishment to the poor people who feed their swine.

These two polemical powers may be combined in various proportions: the philosophical disputant may have more or less wit; the poetical may at times introduce more or less of argument; whereof the *Clouds* furnish a classical example. Yet, if judicious, he will try to keep as much as may be within the region of the ridiculous, and not to manifest his skill by delineating what is loathsome. Prodigious cleverness may be displayed in such a delineation: it may make one turn half sick with disgust: but the poet's aim is not to disgust, but to delight, to exhibit what he alone duly sees and thoroughly feels, the everlasting indissoluble alliance between beauty and truth, between goodness and gladness. We have been told over and over again, that the business of poetry is to please: it is so, and this is the cause: the wisdom of the Imagination is clothed in smiles; she leaves frowns to the weekday faculties of the soul. A purely hateful character, such as Shelley has represented in his *Cenci*; a work surpassingly excellent for the chaste beauty of its diction, is an unpoetical character. The poet averts or rather diverts us from evil, not by stamping on it and treading out its venomous entrails, but in a quieter and pleasanter way, by widening that smile of rapture which it is his high privilege to excite, into a laugh; by shewing the weaknesses of human nature, but without uncovering its nakedness or disgracing it: on the contrary he leaves us with an intenser love for what is good therein, and a more ardent devotion to its welfare. The historian may drain and strain the English tongue, and write till his style cracks and his orthography gets the cramp, in abuse of the Athenian commonwealth: Aristophanes neither strains nor grows hoarse, but awakens the jocund spirits of laughter. No one so powerfully exposes all that is bad in Athens; and yet who ever loved Athens more than Aristophanes? what image is the presiding hearth-god of his works, what idea is breathed into us by every line he has left, but that of the city which, with all its failings, none else can rival or approach? So again the essayist, with a mind as plain although it may not be so spacious as Hounslow heath, and with thoughts as distinct and perchance as numerous as his fingers, will declaim against the silliness of chivalry, if he can think of no fresher topic on which to vent his bile and his self-satisfaction. He will talk about ignorance, and darkness, and absurdity, and folly, and the like, such being perhaps the qualities he is most familiar with; and he will congratulate himself on being born in an age when knight-errantry has been supplanted by author-vagrancy, when magazines contain anything but armour, and when a youthful aspirant after renown, instead of breaking a lance in a tournament, wears a quill to the stump in a review. It was in a far different spirit that the chivalrous Cervantes, when the light of chivalry was expiring, put his extinguisher on it, and drove away the moths that alone still fluttered around it. He loved chivalry too well, to be patient when he saw it parodied and burlesqued; and he perceived that the best way of preserving it from shame, was, to throw over it the sanctity of death. And yet, when he set up his scare-crow, how many chivalrous virtues he could not refrain from investing him with! Here again we are won away from an error, and still retain our admiration of the principle which in its decrepitude so corrupted itself.

U.

Dwarfs strut: giants stoop.   U.

What is the use of ridicule? To point out the deformity of foolish things to the fancy; as the use of reasoning is to demonstrate their foolishness to the understanding. That a mere intellectualist should object to such a weapon, does not surprise me. He who would proscribe a sense of beauty for attracting without formal proof, may consistently condemn ridicule, because there too the proof is informal. But for poets to cry out against it—and many do—only shews them to be nothing more than half poets.

It was a matter of boast to the Romans, that they invented a new species of poetry, the satire. The fact, I believe, is so; and the reason is plain. The Greeks were incapable of inventing anything so unpoetical. Their Satyrs haunted the woods, and were beings among whom the Imagination could be content to abide, even as Una abode amongst them, without disparagement to her heavenly purity, taming their wildness and softening their ferocity, and breathing something of a human soul into these anti-genii, or concentrations of the animal nature. Whereas the Roman satires have no scent of the woods; their haunts are the purlieus of sin: in Juvenal they reached their full impurity, and in him they are the toadstools that spring up in the hotbed of corruption. U.

A good razor never hurts or scratches. Neither would good wit, were men as tractable as their chins. But instead of parting with our intellectual bristles quietly, we set them up and wriggle. Who can wonder then if we are cut to the bone? and however ridiculous lather alone may make us look, lather shot with blood makes us look much more so.

After all, wit is an edged tool. It is well to have it: but take care how you use it. Else it may wound your neighbour; it may cut your own finger, or even your throat. U.

Nobody can be such an enemy to another, as almost every body is to himself.   u.

Far the greater number of mankind spend their lives in making themselves miserable. A great many are chiefly employed in making others miserable. Not a few, thank God! busy themselves a good deal about making others happy. The only rarities are the persons who make themselves happy.

This is very odd: for everybody says, nobody thinks of or cares about anybody half so much as himself.

What if that should be the very reason?

u.

You love good: shew your love, by your activity and unweariedness in wooing and trying to win it, by watching all its motions and slightest gestures, by laying wait for its going out and its coming in, by sitting all night long under its window, if perchance you may hear its voice or catch the light of its face, by diligently seeking for it in every thing that befalls you, by aiming at it and keeping its image before you in every thing you do, by tracing its footsteps and its spirit in every thing your neighbour does.

There is hardly anything which you may not turn to good, even as there is nothing which the sun cannot illuminate. It is the simplest of all metamorphoses, and, when you are used to it, almost the easiest : only set about it heartily. *L'appetit vient en mangeant,* as the French say. This in short is the true philosopher's stone; it changes all things into what is far more precious than gold, into that of which gold is only one of the utensils; and it may be found. v.

Certain mathematical theorems hold equally as moral truths : only few people acknowledge, and still fewer discern, their evidence and unquestionableness, when they are applied to spiritual things. Men are very slow to believe that the right road is the right road, or that the straight path to any point is the shortest: everybody whispers in your ear that he has found out a short cut of his own, and is ready to shew it you, if you will but follow him and keep his secret: for else all the inns will be full, and there will be no getting horses. In spite of this, everybody is angry with all the rest of the world, for not treading in the same track with himself, for not doing exactly as he does. In this most reasonable anger all agree; but in few things besides. Yet I cannot feel sure that this world would be a much better place, although men were like pins or nine-pins, multiplicates of each other. True, we are or ought all to be moving toward the same point; but that point is a centre toward which we are converging:

for the present we stand at different points in the circumference, it matters not whether of the same, or of divers concentric circles; and although your business is to make for the goal along your radius, your neighbour's nearest way lies along his. Therefore quarrel not with your neighbour because his temper is not your temper, nor his understanding your understanding, nor his pursuits your pursuits: rather admire the inexhaustible opulence of nature, bringing forth such a crowd and throng of creatures all differing in kind, but all precious and wholesome, if so be they fulfil the duties of their kind.

But you wish to give your brother your arm, and to help him on? Perhaps during a long journey men walk better with their arms free. I say men: because I know not that it is true of women: their arms seem to seek a resting-place; and the comfort thus given to the heart, may more than make amends for any trifling hinderance to the body.

But you want to have your brother near you, and to shake hands with him? Make haste then and get to the centre, and be ready there to welcome him on his arrival. U.

Finding fault must have something strangely agreeable, seeing that so many spend in it the largest part of their lives. Success to be sure encourages them: in hunting for faults, nobody is ever at a fault. The odd thing is, that, the employment being so delightful, no one ever thinks of carrying it on at home, where it would cost far less trouble. Perhaps people are used to see so much good within doors, that when they go abroad it sickens them, and they want a little refreshing variety. They warm themselves before their own fire, but can only wind the smoke out of another's chimney. And yet a person may turn his own dunghill to some profit, while his neighbour's can only annoy him, especially if he thrusts his nose into it. For my own part I would rather go into my neighbour's garden, and smell the choicest flowers or taste the choicest fruit there: they are likely to be pleasanter and sweeter.

U.

Learned men have objected to deriving *lucus a non lucendo*, from the want, they say, of any like etymology. That suggested by a celebrated divine, of *pancake* from πᾶν κακὸν, is not quite certain. But surely *scandal* is an instance in point: for it means what nobody stumbles or takes offence at, what on the contrary every body picks up and pockets, unless indeed he rather hang it to his watch-ribband and jingle it against his seals.

U.

It is the beam that is censorious: the poor little mote is shame-faced and silent. I think of this, when I hear the men of the eighteenth or nineteenth century inveying against the follies of the twelfth or the sixteenth. They did not treat us so. U.

The intellectual soul has many senses or members, by which it communicates with the outward world, but which yet are no more the intellect itself, than the limbs of the body are the life. Such are memory and attention, which last however is rather a habit than a faculty; such also are the powers of expression and perception; fancy, with which, as with an eye, we see similitudes; apprehension, with which, as with a hand, we lay hold on objects and notions; and lastly sense, as it is familiarly called, by which we practically discover of two instruments which is the more suitable, of two actions which is the more expedient. Each of these faculties is susceptible of various excellencies, and these excellencies are all so many talents.

Genius on the other hand is a perfection of the soul itself. But what perfection? For the soul not only thinks, it also feels and wills. Now these its parts should not live in unneighbourly separation, but should endeavour to become one, as far as may be, by interpenetration and interfusion. The condition of the soul is then most perfect, when the intellect is impassioned, the passions intellectualized, and both are elevated, refined, controuled, actuated, and directed by a master principle. And this interpenetration and interfusion, I conceive, form the essence of Genius. Its most remarkable property or organ is its digestion, whereby it assimilates all things; and its chief instinct is to realize an idea.

Let me follow out my brother's remark: for he seems to me to have caught sight of the truth, in a matter of no little obscurity and perplexity. Coleridge has often tried to lay down certain distinctions between Talent and Genius, in *the Friend*, (*Vol.* i, *p.* 183. *Vol.* iii, *pp.* 78, 85.) and elsewhere; and has displayed his usual ingenuity for discovering the invisible and tracing the furthest and finest ramifications of an idea. Yet, so far as I can judge, he has not satisfied others of the essential difference in their nature: and this want of success I would attribute to his having chiefly delineated what is remote and derivative, if it be not accidental, without digging into the ground and pulling up the root. It is true, the common eye best distinguishes a tree by its leaves; but the scientific eye would see the root, would examine the seed, would search until it discerned the miniature of the oak in the acorn. If you want a person to possess an idea fully, put him fully in possession of it. What we have once known thoroughly, we never lose; what we have not, was never ours. The light on the glow-worm passes away: the light in the diamond endures as long as the diamond.

Nay more, I cannot help doubting whether Mr. Coleridge himself ever reached the origin of the difference: had he done so, he would hardly have talked about *talent*, or used the vulgar phrase *a man of talent*. Landor, although no professing metaphysician, yet guided by that tact for propriety in language, which characterizes him almost above every other writer I am acquainted with, has reproved this expression in his interesting and instructive dialogue between Johnson and Tooke (*Imag. Conv.* Vol. ii. *p.* 213.) which all desirous of writing English ought to know by heart. In this instance, as in others where a word has been fingered and thumbed until its meaning is effaced, a thing especially frequent in abstract terms and the names of spiritual things, since the commonalty, never having framed a precise notion of their value, let 'them rub against the larger and harder copper coins, and are often glad to pass them off, as the Irishman passed off his guinea, between two half-pence; in such cases, to restore the original impression, one must try to recover the original die. 'He who wishes to define an ambiguous word, ought to shew that the signification he assigns to it is not arbitrary, by shewing it to be consistent with etymology, or with analogy, or with primitive usage.

Now there is little question that the common use of the word *talent* to denote a faculty of the mind, is traceable to the parable of the talents in the New Testament: just as many other words, *lazar* for example, spring from the same source: just as *parole* and *palabra* (whence our *palaver*, in derision perhaps of what was deemed a Spanish peculiarity) are only forms of παραβολή, and must at first have meant the word of the Saviour. The true sense of the parable was evident: the talents were spiritual gifts or endowments: so wherever any spiritual or intellectual faculty existed in a high degree, it was called a talent. A good memory was a talent; an eye for painting was a talent; a musical ear was a talent; readiness of speech was a talent; a man might have a talent for raillery, a talent for logic: " Horace (says Dryden,) is to be considered in his three different talents, as a critic, satirist, and writer of odes." All the other instances cited by Johnson prove that this is the old and right usage. The original meaning of the word in France, whence we probably imported it, was the same. All these talents were so many gifts, so many *dons*, names often applied to them. They were, so to say, the particular features or members of the mind, when any-wise eminent or remarkable: so that the excellence of any faculty is a talent. But as a face may have fine eyes without a handsome nose or mouth, so the possession of one talent implies not the possession of another. Hence it is a blunder to club them together, and denominate the whole flock by a singular noun. A man may have a talent of a particular kind; he may have several talents of particular kinds; amassing them we may say he has talents, or is a man of talents; but he can no more have talent or be a man of talent, than he can have pound or be a man of po u d, than he can have letter or be a man of letter.

Genius on the other hand is one and whole and indivisible. We cannot say that a man has geniuses, as we ought not to say that he has talent. Shakspeare was a man of genius; but even Shakspeare was not a man of geniuses. Genius is the excellence of the soul itself as an intelligence. It is that central pervading essence which modifies and regulates and determines all the particular faculties; it is above the soul and in the soul and one with it: as the talents are its executive ministry and may be many, so genius being its legislative principle can only be one. And as, when governments are disordered, the harmony between the administration and the principle of law is at an end, so in the diseased and broken state of our nature the harmony between its genius and its talents ceases, and the voice of genius seems to speak to us from without, even as the voice of conscience seems to speak; or rather the voice proceeds from a self-within ourselves, from that holy place which we have forfeited the privilege of entering, and into which we can only obtain admission again through the reconciling blood of the atonement. Hence it is that men of genius have looked on their genius as something distinct from themselves: like conscience, it is seated behind the veil which our will by its wilfulness draws across the soul; and the will cannot controul it, cannot add to it or take away from it, cannot command it to do this or that; it is what it is, and such it continues to be: let it act freely, and its might is almost boundless, and its offspring are almost everlasting; chain or curb it, and it is nothing. Hence was it that Socrates spoke of his genius as of a δαιμόνιον or supernatural power. Hence too the very name of genius.

But alas! while talents are things which can be handled and talked about, I feel that genius can only be fully understood or intelligibly described by him who possesses it; and he perhaps must rather represent than describe it. Yet these scanty observations may help some to more accurate notions on this difficult subject. Nothing can be vaguer or more turbid than the common use of the two words. People feel that there is a difference between them: the most slovenly writer would hardly call Milton a man of talent, or Waller a man of genius: but this feeling gropes about blindly, without seeing its own reasonableness: so, after the usual practice of our helpless understanding, which, when at variance with the imagination, likes to bring all things under the simplest category, that of quantity, and knowing nothing of the essential dogmatizes about the formal, and incapable of recognizing any distinction of nature, will hear of nothing but a difference as to *more* or *less;* here likewise the general opinion is, that talent is a lower degree of genius, and genius a higher degree of talent, even as monkeyhood is a lower humanity, and humanity a higher monkeyhood. u.

There is no commoner stopgap in conversation than such questions as *Which do you think the best play of Shakspeare?* or *the best novel of Walter Scott?* Yet among all the questions which the schoolmen tried to solve in their logical crucible, and wherewith the modern scorners of logic have stilled the cravings of their vanity and tickled themselves into a dull forced laugh, none, not even the famed one about the number of angels who can dance on the point of a needle, is not quite as rational and answerable. Indeed the paralogism in the two cases is the same:

the modes of space and number are applied to things with which space and number have nothing to do. The pinnacle of Strasburg Minster may be a certain number of feet higher than the cross of St. Peter's; the cubic content of St. Peter's may exceed by a certain number of feet that of Strasburg Minster: these are points which may be ascertained by measurement. But where shall we learn that intellectual trigonometry which will determine whether Lear or Macbeth be the sublimer tragedy? whether a Gothic cathedral or a Grecian temple be the grander building? or, to make the absurdity more palpable, which is the most beautiful, the Iliad, the Parthenon, Cleopatra, Mont Blanc, the vale of Tempe, a palm-tree, or a rose-bud? A different idea of beauty, or, if the idea be one, a different modification of it, has become manifest in every one of these objects; and ideas or manifestations of ideas differ not quantitively, but specifically or generically: so that the office of the Judgement or Critical Faculty is to examine with what completeness any particular idea is embodied and revealed in its earthly form, not to weigh or measure different ideas against one another. In other words, every object is to be judged of by itself, not by others; and the business of Judgement is with the positive, not with the comparative or superlative.

Landor indeed, in his dialogue between Southey and Porson (p. 69), speaks of such intellectual trigonometry, only however as a thing desirable, not as having actual existence: nor is it likely to have any, seeing it is a notional nonentity. He also complains more than once that " no critic has ever been able to fix the exact degrees of excellence above a certain point :" the failure is owing to the impossibility of the thing attempted. But impossibilities are ot to be attempted with impunity: the teeth which gnaw at a piece of iron, wear themselves away. Criticism would not be in its present deplorable reptile state, unless critics had wasted their faculties in striving to do what is not to be done. Nor are books the only sufferers by those odious things, comparisons. We seem incapable of admiring anything, without at the same time disparaging something else: even Wordsworth in some fine lines already quoted says that " the beauty of promise sets the budding rose above the rose full-blown." The rose-bud would blush with shame at the preference: true, it has this peculiar beauty; still it cannot be said that in every sense youth is more beautiful than age, promise than fulfilment, the bud than the flower, morning than day and evening and night, spring than summer and autumn. We are indeed for ever exalting some one of these above what we are pleased to deem its rival, although nothing like rivality severs them; but our reasons for doing so are altogether arbitrary, and depend on the casual changing whim of the moment. Hear Wordsworth again in an autumnal sonnet:

> This rustling dry
> Through the green leaves, and yon crystalline sky,
> Announce a season potent to renew
> Mid frost and snow the instinctive joys of song,
> And nobler cares than listless summer knew.

It is really hard that winter cannot be praised, without abusing summer in the same breath; that they cannot be allowed to exist side by side in our thoughts, as they exist in nature, in sisterly beauty and amity; that we cannot smile on the favorite of the moment, without frowning askance on every other woman in the room. But so it is: we are the slaves of a domineering egotistical understanding, which will not let us wander freely, enjoying the flowers as they bloom beside our path, and alive to every joyous impression, but compels us to make a choice, to subscribe certain articles of faith, and then resolves that everything, except that whereon it sheds the light of its countenance, must be worthless.

From these considerations it appears, that precipitancy in pronouncing one book better or worse than another, indicates not superior discernment of their relative merits, but a feeble discernment of their positive merits.   υ.

The reason why many people are so fond of using superlatives, is, they are so positive that the poor positive is not half positive enough for them.   υ.

Poor Richard! all his geese are swans.
Doubly poor Robert! all his swans are geese.
   υ.

How many merits one sees in those one likes! how many faults in those one dislikes! Yet people fancy they see with their eyes.   υ.

All our senses have their imported prejudices, and adopt and lay aside and alter their tastes at foreign example and suggestion: a proof that even in ordinary men the mind modifies the senses more directly, not to say (which I believe I might so far as appears) more, than the senses modify the mind.

Hardly a writer does not use a magnifying glass. U.

I once heard a woman say to her husband, after several little controversies playfully carried on and prettily declined: *Je ne sais pas comment il arrive, mais tu as toujours raison.* This speech delighted and surprised me: others I hope will only be delighted by it.

The opposite speech in the play is well known; and that would never have surprised anybody.

U.

—Doribert is the first person in the universe.

Are you quite sure of it?

To be sure.....By the by, do you know, there is not a question on which we do not think exactly alike.

I heard him speak slightingly of your favorite Johnson the other day.

Oh! I was always certain that he did not know a good book from a bad.

This barefacedness of our self-love thrusting its head through our esteem for others, may be rare: cover it up a little, and nothing is commoner. u.

Time delights in contradictions. When it passes slowly, it is gone very fast; and when shortest in its presence, it is longest in the retrospect. u.

Physical objects are lessened by distance; moral objects are often magnified by it. Most pleasures are greater in forethought or afterthought than in enjoyment; and a danger anticipated is far more dreadful than a danger encountered. u.

. Puppies are blind: I suppose, because their eyes are looking inward. u.

Vanity is vanity. u.

You who prate so glibly and so thoughtlessly about giving a nation a constitution, believe me, you might as reasonably talk about giving a man a constitution. It were a lighter matter to transport London with its double cathedral into Africa, than to carry thither our constitution with its two houses of Parliament. A constitution is the child of Time, the mate of Life, the disciple of Necessity, the ward of Providence. If none but God can breathe a soul into a man, neither can any but God breathe a soul into a people. u.

It was the original sentence on mankind, that whatever we bring forth should be brought forth with pain, that the human race should be fed by the labour of the man, and should increase and multiply by the labour of the woman, that our bread should be moistened with the sweat of the brow, and that we should come into the world amid groans and tears. So is it likewise with the human race. The sweat must have run down the cheeks of a nation, before its condition can be bettered: the world must be in labour, before it can bring forth happiness: and unless our own sins render our pains abortive, every succeeding revolution will be as it were a throe of childbirth. U.

Light, when suddenly let in, dazzles and hurts and almost blinds us: but this soon passes away, and it seems to become the only element we can exist in.

Statesmen ought to define their objects fully and conclusively within their own minds, before they engage in active life. Else their actions may get to shape their principles, instead of their principles shaping their actions.

———

The knowledge of one's strength doubles it: the ignorance of it halves it. u.

———

On peut savoir tout sans savoir faire. u.

———

At the wonder-match in the fairy tale, the prince produces a nut, out of which he draws I know not how many yards of muslin. Any Spaniard five years since would have beat him hollow: he would have pulled out of his waistcoat pocket the whole constitution of his country, perhaps still more finely spun, and almost as durable. u.

———

The business of a statesman is to deal with

men. This has been lost sight of by most of our recent legislators and constitution-mongers: or they must have drawn their notion of men from the chess-board, and have fancied moreover that they were themselves playing both sets: a kind of game which commonly ends in a puzzle, and in both parties having the worst of it: so unbecoming is it to other things as well as the Thames, to have their two sides on one side. Would you see how men are not to be dealt with? read any of the French Constitutions, or the Spanish: They are all based on the same fundamental error, the fancy that a forest will spring up if you only mumble over a few pages of Linnæus. Would you on the other hand behold how a true statesman deals with men such as they are, having flesh and blood and all the good and evil that flesh and blood are heirs to? how he breaks them in and manages and controuls them, but without maiming their strength or quenching their spirit? with how gentle a hand he disentangles the fruit-bearing plant from the noxious creeper that is stifling it? how he searches for every little islanded spot of good ground to sow his good seed in? how kind he is, how condescending, how indulgent, and how he displays the consciousness of his own superiority chiefly by the silent acknowledgement that he has no right to expect from others what he has a duty to exact from himself? how in fine he prepares and accomplishes the blessed task of bringing the confused elements of society into order, and where hatred and rapine and bloodshedding and terror have been raging, there makes peace grow and joy and confidence and that love which arises when families dwell together in amity? would you see and understand how all this is to be done, read Sir John Malcolm's *Instructions to his Assistants and Officers*, and his account of his administration in Central India: read and see how much may be effected, even in four short years, when a man sets about it rightly and wisely. U.

Tibi impera. Deo pare. Hominibus, sicuti Naturæ, parendo impera. U.

———

Dieu seul peut commencer par le commencement. U.

———

Is not straitening the best way of straightening? Look into a foul clothes' bag and see: it will serve just as well as a crowded prison, or an election mob. True, clean linen packs closely: but then it is clean. And though ironing and mangling are good for shirts, I am not sure that they are equally good for the wearers; notwithstanding the authority of sundry rulers, who seem to have served their apprenticeship in the laundry. U.

———

People cannot go wrong, if you don't let them. They cannot go right, unless you let them. U.

The great discovery of modern statecraft, is, that policy means police.   U.

I hate to see trees pollarded .. or nations.

    U.

Lisping must be very common: so many people call royalty loyalty.   U.

The very idea of lawful Power involves the prior existence of Law, through its conformity with which alone can Power become lawful.

    U.

It is quite right that there should be a heavy duty on cards: not only on moral grounds; not only because they act on a social party like a torpedo, silencing the merry voice and numbing the play of the features; not only to still the hunger of the public purse, which, reversing the qualities of Fortunatus's, is always empty, however much you may put into it; but also because every pack of cards is a malicious libel on courts, and on the world, seeing that the trumpery, with number one at the head, is the best part of them, and that it gives kings and queens no other companions than knaves.

U.

When the spirit of good is busy, the spirit of evil is not idle. This has been made manifest at every momentous epoch in history. So likewise has the converse, expressed in the German proverb:

> When need is highest,
> Then aid is nighest.   U.

Even folly has its use. The cackling of geese has more than once saved the capitol. Tetzel awakened Luther.

U.

What would be the state of the world, if God did not bring good out of evil? He may do this: man cannot. It is true, man tries, or would persuade others and even himself that he tries: but it is like a wasp's trying to fly through a pot of honey. U.

Oxenstiern's son, on his arrival at the congress of Munster, dismayed by the gravity of the Spanish plenipotentiaries, and by the quickness and ready confidence of the French, wrote to beg that his father would send him some sage and experienced adviser. The great chancellor's answer is well known: *Mi Fili, parvo mundus regitur intellectu.* He spake with reference to the policies and ordinances of man: and the histories of two thousand years are comments on his remark. But men, in their conscious intelligent agency, have not much more to do with the government of the world, than they have to do with the motion of the earth; whereat if all its inhabitants amassing their whole strength were to push for a century, they could not even shake it in its stedfast course.

In the mighty watch of our world, which hath the moon for its month-hand, and the sun for its year-hand, man at the utmost is only the mainspring, needing to be perpetually wound up as the chain of life runs out, going right only so long as he meekly fulfils the purpose of his maker, but evermore liable to be disordered by the strain or shock of his passions or the intrusive dirt of his sensuality. Oxenstiern spake truly, inasmuch as he spake of man; whose intellect, seldom very strong, save in his own conception, has usually grown giddy on mounting any lofty eminence of power. Had Oxenstiern spoken with reference to the true Governor of the world, he would have said: *Magno mundus regitur intellectu*. Wherever science has traced his footsteps, it has discovered that Infinite Power is the executive of Infinite Wisdom. It has perceived this in all those lower orders of things which it is better able to survey: and if the same is not equally evident in contemplating mankind, it is because the object is so gigantic that the eye cannot comprehend it, and thus cannot discern the relative proportion and reciprocal adaptation of its parts; because man collectively, as individually, cannot see the whole of himself. All that we behold is a mere fragment, as it were a Torso of the colossal statue; and the beauty of such a fragment is hardly perceivable, except where the Imagination can supply what is wanting.

Let me observe here that the contrast between Oxenstiern and the contemporaneous minister of France, Mazarin, aptly illustrates the difference remarked above between third-thoughted and second-thoughted men. Mazarin was palsied by his prudence. Oxenstiern was no less prudent; but his prudence combined with his generosity to constitute magnanimity: and as he reconciled his first and second thoughts in his third, so Gustavus Adolphus may perhaps serve as an example of one who anticipated his second thoughts in his first. Hardly any other hero has been so politic; hardly any other politician has been so heroic: nor can any rhyme in Terza Rima be more perfect than was the harmony between the great king and his great minister.   U.

When we skim along the surface of history, we see little but the rough barren rocks that rise out of it.   U.

Did we duly consider how far the goodness of a single individual may be influential in his neighbourhood, how that influence may be propagated in ever-widening circles, and may ultimately in no small degree promote the welfare of his country, it would surely be a great support and strengthening to our weak faltering virtue. If ten righteous men had been found in the city, Sodom would have been spared: indeed it could hardly have been Sodom:

but among ten every unit is important. The kingdom of heaven, we know, is as a grain of mustard seed; and whatever belongs to that kingdom, is in like manner fruitful. υ.

Nothings bears interest to a wise man, except principle.

To be sure! says a broker: what else should? υ.

Où trouvera-t-on des gens comme il faut?
En Paradis.
Mais il n'y a là que des parvenus.
A la bonne heure: donc à Paris. υ.

Heroism would not be heroism, did not half the world mistake it for superstition or infidelity or treason or madness or folly.

The only way of undoing the Gordian knot of circumstances is that which Alexander tried, by decision. He knew it to be the rapidest kind of resolution. That single deed marked him out as the man born to cut through not only the twisted policies of Greece, but also that still more thickly ravelled complication in which the destinies of Greece and Asia had been involved for two centuries, and wherein the swords of Marathon and Salamis and Platea had only made a rent. 'As soon however as the disentangler was gone, the entangling began anew; only the thread was finer and still brittler. At length the iron foot of the Romans stamped on it and mashed it.'

By the only way, I mean the only way in action, not in speculation: for the actor finds, the thinker seeks: the former lays hold on one thing, the latter takes a survey of many. Alexander's teacher went otherwise to work: his *Organon* was not the sword: he tried to analyse, that is, to untie the knot, and his writings are the Journal of his progress. The legend indeed tells that he at last bethought himself of copying his pupil, but that like most copyists he marred his model, by throwing himself into the inextricable Euripus. If there be any thing like truth in the story, it must be interpreted differently. The ebb and flow which puzzled him, were not the ebb and flow of waters: his Euripus was upon the earth; its current was fate; the same current into which Demosthenes plunged in the selfsame year, and into which three centuries afterward the last of the Romans plunged at Utica for the selfsame reason.

No less emblematic than what Alexander did, as well of his character as of his destiny, was Napoleon's behaviour at Milan, when he took the iron crown from the archbishop and himself placed it on his own head. He took everything; he would receive nothing, not even a blessing: so he had to fight foes against which nothing but blessings can prevail, curses; and they were too much for him. u.

What ought to have been done, and what shall be done, often stifle doing between them.

———

I doubt whether the Duke of Wellington himself could move a company of ordinary persons rapidly from the drawing-room into the dining-room: nobody will go first. Were it so in the world, society would be always at a standstill. A master-mind is wanted to shew the way.

———

Que doit on faire dans ce bas monde?
On doit dîner.
Et puis?
Badiner.   u.

———

Hors d'œuvres become made dishes in England; in the drawing-room and the library, as well as in the kitchen.   u.

———

It must be very unnatural to be natural; few people being so, except naturals.   u.

How easy it is to pass sentence against a work! All we understand in it, is common-place: all we understand not is nonsense. *u.*

What are the books of philosophers? Mostly windfalls from the tree of knowledge. *u.*

Some vermin are begotten and born and beget and die in a day. Literature has similar vermin. One might indeed doubt about the third point: but like breeds like. *u.*

There can be no shade without light. Ignorance would never have been discovered to be among us, had it not been pointed out by knowledge. So is it with negatives universally: they owe, many of them their existence, all of them our perception of it, to the qualities of which they are negations. But if positives lead us to observe negatives, they in return best teach us the nature and value of positives. This is one reason why the perfection of male virtue is likely to be stronger than the perfection of female. It has added to truth knowledge, and is not only founded on a conviction of the goodness of what is good, but is likewise guarded on every side by the discernment of the evil of what is evil.

There can be no shade then without light. Now what is shade? The exclusion of light from a given spot by the accidental intervention of a dark body; the dimness, for example, of a room from which the sun has been partially shut out, or of a deep and narrow glen obscured by an overhanging mountain, or of a wall running east and west where one side is sacrificed to the other. But that which is accidental, is also temporary. After a time the windows will be thrown open, the glen will be lifted up, and a vertical sun will shower his rays on both sides of the wall equally. For though there can be no shade without light, there may and hereafter will be light without shade.

When you speak to a stranger, how are you to address him? I suppose you must *Sir* him. And yet there is something so startling and repelling in that triliteral monosyllable, with its initial hiss and closing rumble, that, used between equals, if it stand alone or prominently, and be not softened down into a scarcely distinguishable enclitic, it seems well-nigh to portend a challenge. I hate the ugly Johnsonian word, and can hardly use, or hear it without repugnance. I would almost as soon throw myself into the vacuum of abstract humanity, and call my neighbour *Man*. The French, with that delicacy of social tact which belongs to them, never separate their appellative from the pronoun, which seeks the individual out of the mass, bringing him into some kind of personal relation to the speaker: and the assaults of jacobinism upon individuality were in this respect vain: *Citoyen* and *Citoyenne* were soon replaced by *Monsieur* and *Madame*.

Would it were as easy to restore all the other good things devoured by that polypus preying on the heart of the body politic! In like manner among the Germans, the friendliest of nations, the vocative *Herr* is seldom uttered without the individualizing humanizing pronoun. And even we use the pronoun to persons of rank. Its absence in Italian might be deemed a type of the disunion which has in all ages distracted that unfortunate, fratricidal and suicidal country, where every man is always fancying that he feels his neighbour's hand at his throat or in his pocket, and where the phantasies and schemes of the Unitarians, as they style themselves, even if all hinderances from without were removed, appear about as feasible as giving consistency to a heap of needles: only Spain offers the same phenomenon. In both countries it is connected with the want in the national character of those gregarious qualities, by the operation of which in England,

France, and Germany, has been gradually developed what by way of eminence we call society, that is to say, a happy conformity and free circulation of manners, customs, and habits, throughout the people, every domestic circle intersecting with numberless others: which same cause explains why the novel of society and manners has no existence in the South of Europe, whereas among the central nations it now forms the chief staple article of fine literature. At all events however there is something in *signor* and *señor* for the voice to dwell on, and by its intonation to indicate sentiment; they have a fulness of sound and a capability of modulated expression, very different from the affronting abruptness of our vowel-less unchangeable *Sir*.

Indeed one can hardly help wishing at times to be a Southron, for the sake of being called by a southern name. Listen to the names which meet you at every turn and winding in a Spanish chronicle: many of them come upon you with a sweeping sound, like a full peal of bells, while others have a depth and a solemnity as if they were brooding over the glory they had inherited from "Pelayo and the Campeador." Look at the names of the historians themselves, Juan Mariana, Geronymo Zurita, Antonio de Herrera y Tordesillas, Vicente Bacallar y Saña, Antonio de Solis y Ribadeneyra. Such names are worth having; the breath that pronounces them is not wasted. But as for the mincing, minikin, make-believe sounds, David Hume, William Robertson, Edward Gibbon, one might as well be denominated by numerals or algebraic symbols, and called 155 or xz^2. What a name has Shakspeare given to his lover! Romeo: and how Juliet loves it! how she "makes Echo's airy tongue grow hoarse with repetition of her Romeo's name!" The first sounds in which she breathes her passion into the ear of night, are, "O Romeo, Romeo, wherefore art thou Romeo!" It would be a mistake to suppose that nothing is meant in this and the following lines, except a wish that her lover had another name: the name that drives him from her, is not Romeo, but Montague. She would not have it changed for the world: while pretending to chide it, she is regaling herself with its luscious melody: it rests and lingers on her lips, "never ending, still beginning." But what can even the sweetest and fondest voice make of William, or Henry, or Charles, or John, or Smith, or Thompson, or Simpkins, or Bankes? Many a time must the *dearest Robert,* the *beloved Wiggins,* the *adorable Ash,* have wished that he belonged to that numerous family of *Anon* who wrote half the *Elegant Extracts.* Change only a few letters in Romeo, and let Juliet exclaim, *O Thomas, Thomas, wherefore art thou Thomas!* and I would stake a ducat to a denier that not one mouth in ten would preserve its rigidity. This is not owing merely to the latter being a common, and therefore a vulgar name: *Mary* is one of the commonest in the world, as common as roses, and still must always be one of the most beautiful. The reason is rather, that in the change the vowels are lost; and a pack of consonants may indeed be arranged rhythmically and harmoniously, but have still less melody than a pack of hounds. Hence also even our best names, such as Herbert, Percy, Pembroke, Talbot, Stanley, Gordon, Campbell, owe far more of their value to the associations and recollections connected with them, than to their sound; although the liquids or, as they are not unaptly termed, semivowels, which in all these names are the emphatic letters, admit in some degree of prolongation and intonation. It is the same in our sweetest female names, Emily, Emmeline, Ellen, Fanny, Margaret, Dorothea, Genevieve, Rosalind, Imogen, Miranda, Ophelia, Perdita: the important consonants are all liquids; as they are likewise in ἔρως, *amor,* and its modern derivatives, in *minne, liebe, love,* in order that the sound may have something in accord with the feeling.

It seems to have arisen from some kind of instinctive consciousness, that admiration and reverence and love, and all our higher and purer feelings, delight to dwell and repose on their objects, and to linger about them, thereby intimating their original and ultimate union with eternity and infinity and peace; while hatred and arrogance and every base and malignant passion are *abrupt* and *concise,* that is literally, break themselves off and cut themselves short, and thus bear witness of the nothingness from which they are struggling to escape, and into which at the same time they appear impatient to return: it seems to be from some instinct of this sort, as well as for the sake of distinction, that in speaking to royalty we have adopted the longer form *Sire.* I might here observe that a like instinct has led the French to address persons of rank with the unabridged *Monseigneur;* I might proceed to notice, that, in spite of the ridicule cast lavishly, because at little expense of thought or wit, on the long German accumulative tit'es, *Hochgeborner, Hochwohlgeborner, Edelsthochwohlgeborner,* and the rest of them, at least they were not the produce of an age and nation whose greatest trouble was how to put themselves to the least trouble; I might further inquire whether any and what qualities in the English character correspond with or illustrate that most inhospitable word *Sir;* and Simond's account of what he saw at the fall of Schaffhausen might serve in lieu of a thousand similar anecdotes: but I remember that, notwithstanding the example set by Berkeley, the inverted pyramid is not yet become an approved style of architecture. u.

It is said by Milton, that " we Englishmen, being far northerly, do not open our mouths in the cold air, wide enough to grace a southern tongue; but are observed by all other nations to speak exceeding close and inward." (*Of Education, Works*, Vol. 1. p. 278). To perceive the truth of this, you need only see an English and Italian singer side by side. The chief study of the former seems, to waste as little breath and to distort her face as little as may be; while the latter unfolds the gates of her mouth and lets the full torrent of sound stream forth. But the operation of the same cause is discernible throughout our language, which it has stript of vowel after vowel, yearly taking from it something of its melody. To be sure, we gain compression: and this would be something, were our thoughts so copious that we could not house them except by squeezing them up closely: but it is not everything: and even in speech it may be doubted whether ice do not take up more room than water; Seneca than Plato; not to mention that water finds readier admission. Sometimes the vowels are utterly got rid of: when one sees ἐλεημοσύνη doubled up into *alms*, one can hardly help thinking of the picture where the devil folds up and pockets Peter Schlemihl's shadow. But more commonly, although we retain the form of them, we throw away the substance, slurring them, and hurrying on to the next consonant. Me-mo-ri-a with its four vowels, becomes mem-o-ry or rather mem'-ry with only the final short one: so i-ma-gi-na-ri-us is converted into im-aj-in-ar-y; and poor *knowledge* goes slipshod as *knolledge*, that it may rhyme, I suppose, with its favorite abode. The like process of envowelling words goes on daily: one hears people beginning to call le-gend lej-end, and te-net ten-et. So that in time we shall perhaps adopt the practice of the Semitic nations, and take to expressing that indistinct ill-defined breathing which keeps our consonants from falling into a heap, by points instead of by characters. Formerly it was denoted in many words by an apostrophe; in giving up which I know not that we have done wisely: a character is an unapt symbol of that which has no character.

The last word reminds me that such peculiarities and idioms in language always correspond with and indicate something peculiar and idiomatic in national character. Every language must be the print of the national mind. No thought can be taken up permanently into that mind, but it will stamp its image in words. De Maistre says well, when maintaining that the languages of savages " sont et ne peuvent être que des débris de langues antiques, ruinées, et dégradées comme les hommes qui les parlent: toute dégradation individuelle ou nationale est sur-le-champ annoncée par une dégradation rigoureusement proportionnelle dans le langage. Comment l'homme pourroit-il perdre une idée ou seulement la rectitude d'une idée sans perdre la parole ou la justesse de la parole qui l'exprime? et comment au contraire pourroit-il penser ou plus ou mieux, sans le manifester sur-le-champ par son langage." (*Soirées de St. Petersbourg,* Vol. 1, p. 82). Hardly any work would be more instructive and entertaining, than one to illustrate this proposition, if executed by a man of learning duly under the discipline of judgement. All thoughtful minds are pleased to detect traces of the way in which habits and manners and opinions imperceptibly frame for themselves exponents in words. Every indication of spiritual action is congenial, and therefore delightful, to the soul. Why is physical science so fascinating? because it breathes order and law and intelligent obedience into what at first sight looks like a confused unruly incomprehensible chaos. Thus in all departments of study there is a joy in catching a glimpse of a principle, in discovering a rule, in beholding things as they stand in the sequence of causation, so that what we have been wont to make use of without knowing how or wherefore, we can now deposit ticketed in the cabinets of the understanding. To take an instance of the connexion just referred to between alterations in practice and in language: how emblematic, as has been remarked, is the modern transfer of *speculation* from philosophy to commerce! it has led me into discussions seemingly interminable, and wherein we only receded from each other, when at last it came out that we had taken different courses, and that while Pythagoras or Leibnitz was my pole-star, my companion was looking at M. Rothschild. So again at a time when the personality of God was an idea almost evanescent in our theology, his name too was going into disuse, except in swearing; and many divines became delicately scrupulous about speaking of him by so familiar a term, and chose rather to hide their shrunken faith within the folds of some misty abstraction, talking about Heaven, or Providence, or the Deity, or the Divinity, and resorting to other such phrases to which neither they nor their hearers or readers could attach any definite meaning.

But not only in the sense and spirit of words, are types to be detected; their outward form and sound are significant. To revisit the point whence we started, even the proportion between the vowels and consonants in a language will shew the relative influence of the feelings and of the understanding over the people who speak it. German grammarians have called consonants the objective, vowels the subjective element of language. As the end of human speech is twofold, to utter feelings and to communicate thoughts, we may reasonably look to find the organs of speech adapted to this double purpose. And we do so find them. The vowels express what is felt: they come more immediately from that part of the body which is less under the dominion of the will: they make the whole melody of speech: the interjections in which our bursting emotions find vent, consist chiefly of vowels, repeated sometimes over and over again, and occasionally kept from running and melting into each other by some recurring consonant. Thus they resemble the notes of beasts and birds, which are mainly vocalic, with the admixture of a consonant or two. Much like these are the languages of savage nations, especially where the climate fosters the luxuriant growth of the feelings. In Hawaii, or Owhyhee, the very name of which is a mess of vowels, one meets with such words as *tavovovovo*; and Mr. Ellis gives the following sentence, *e i ai oe ia ia ae e ao ia*, which he renders *speak now to him by the side that he learn*. In consonants on the other hand, fashioned as they are by those organs about the mouth over which we have a fuller and readier controul, one beholds something like the operation of the formative principle on the raw material of language, the shaping and modifying and combining or syllabling action of the intellect. Now if the natural excellence of man lie in the perfect balance or rather the perfect union of the heart and the head, then surely no nation has ever come so near it as the Greeks: and accordingly in no language is the distribution of the vowels and consonants so fair and equable as in theirs: infinitely various and plastic, it runs over every chord of melodious combination, stopping just where strength becomes too harsh and rugged, and sweetness too cloyingly luscious. The Latin, as was to be expected, has not only substituted a stately monotonousness for the ever flexible rhythm and changing accentuation of the Greek: the consonants also begin to predominate; λέγει becomes *legit,* λέγετε *legitis,* λέγουσι *legunt.*

Quintilian himself says: Latina facundia est ipsis statim sonis durior, quando jucundissimas ex Græcis litteras non habemus, Υ et Φ, quibus nullæ apud eos dulcius spirant; et velut in locum earum succedunt tristes et horridæ, quibus Græcia caret. Quid? quod pleraque nos illa quasi mugiente littera cludimus M: at illi N jucundam et in fine quasi tinnientem illius loco ponunt. (xii. 10). Latin is sonorous however and dignified and imperious, and worthy of the kingly senate: it is the language of all others to write laws in. Even the mugient M, the bull's letter, was not ill suited to a people whose chief business was to strike terror. By the modern Italians the speech of their forefathers has been diluted and effeminated, until it has become as feeble as themselves. One hears it called indeed the language of love; but then it must be of sensual voluptuous unstable transient love, not of loyalty and chaste constancy, not of that love in which the imaginative reason consecrates and gives permanence to the animal passion of the moment. These feelings receive their consistency from the intellect; and they are not to be uttered by a mere flux of vowels, but require consonants to hold and bind them together. Now as in English the consonants are too predominant, so are the vowels in Italian. Almost every final consonant has been removed, not always after the usual mode, by rubbing them off, but often by subjoining a vowel, or, what amounts to the same, by setting one of the oblique cases in the place of the theme: ε *sedes* becomes *sedia, parens parente.* Termination too after termination is appended, until one gets to such words as *piacevolissimamente,* with tails as long as the train of a lady's court-dress, and about as unfit for the household business of everyday life; in which moreover the substance is so lost in the attributes, as greatly hinders clear straightforward independent thought. Where every word is in the superlative, it matters little which is chosen: one cannot mean a great deal more or a great deal less than another. In Dante's time this process of unmanning and degradation was still incomplete: he put forth his mighty hand to arrest it: he tried to lift up the prostrate body of his country, to nerve her flaccid limbs, and enable her to stand firmly and lastingly: but he tried in vain. The poison of pleasure spread through her whole frame, relaxing every fibre and sinew, now that it was not resisted by the healthful check of political activity, now that she was become, as he calls her, "Non donna di province, ma bordello." It is interesting to see how Dante likewise strives to brace and strengthen the language, to counteract its luscious softness, to give it something of manly dignity and wholesome asperity, and to form it into a car fit to bear brave and noble thoughts on the field in which Good and Evil are battling, instead of what it now is; a cushioned velvet-lined coach for women and men more womanish than women to loll in down the Corso. The French on the contrary have clipt and trimmed their tongue so that all fulness and majesty and variety of sound have passed away from it: they have broken up their words, as Macadam breaks stones, to make a road for conversation to glide along easily. And they have achieved what they wished: as at their *restaurants*, whatever you can want is ready in a moment: but all is so disguised, you are puzzled to tell what it may once have been; there are no solid substantial joints; and if anything is served up in its natural shape, it is overdone. They never accentuate their words, or their feelings: all is in the same key: a cap is *charmant*, so is Raphael's Transfiguration. Admirably adapted for all the ends of society, so as sometimes even to put *bon mots* into the mouth of those, who in their own language had always kept good things at a distance, it is of little worth for any other purpose. But then society is all in all with the French. I was once pointing out the features of a beautiful prospect to a lady: she listened listlessly, and replied, *Oui, mais il n'y a point de maisons.* She spoke as the representative of her nation. In Spanish one finds a dignity not inferior to the Roman, and at the same time a sweetness ennobled by its alliance with that dignity; even its gutturals give it an inwardness of tone, so that it seems fitted, as Charles the Fifth said, above other languages for the outpourings of the spirit to Heaven. The primary character of all the Teutonic dialects is different: in them the consonants always assert their preeminence; and the wildness and complexity of their intellectual combinations answer well to the constraint of the vocal organs when twisting the uncouthest knots of consonants. It is true, sundry distinctive shades are found in particular nations: we for example have not only cast away from us the euphonous vowels of the Latin, but also in many instances, as in *night* and the like, the accumulated consonants of the German. That is, we endeavour to keep a sound judicious mean, shunning equally the vagrancy of sense, and the vagaries of intellect. How far we have been successful, let others determine. U.

———

A practical maxim results from what has been just said. Inasmuch as vowels, like feelings, may be indefinitely prolonged, while consonants are yet more fleeting and momentary than thoughts; English poets who write for song, should study to introduce as many syllables as they can with full distinct sonorous vowels, especially in those places where the voice is meant to dwell. The neglect of this sometimes throws our singers off their balance, just as if they were trying to support themselves by the leaf of an acacia. U.

———

A minute may be minute; yet every moment is of moment.

Would it not be more appropriate to call articles particles, and particles articles?　u.

Our will, when at twain with reason, lessens all things down to its own littleness. Whatever it insists on, it makes a point of.　u.

People are hardly so tenacious of any rights, as of those which are wrongs.　u.

It is an old remark that we talk less of our good than of our ill health. Perhaps generally we are less talkative in pleasure than in pain; it being the essence of satisfaction to enjoy in peace and tranquillity, while dissatisfaction is ever querulous and garrulous: one cannot grumble without grumbling. When the motion of a carriage is noiseless, we know that all its springs are in order, and that its path is over soft turf: but when things go wrong, it rumbles and creaks, sometimes no less shrilly than an old shrew. A smile is voiceless, a shriek vociferous. Afterwards however all this is reversed: we forget our past pangs and tears, and the sorrows we have gone through, save that about them which was interesting or 'soothing,' and our thoughts and our words linger and abide among the pleasures and smiles of former days. U.

———

A great man commonly disappoints those who visit him. They are on the look-out for his thundering and lightning, and he speaks about common things much like other people; nay sometimes he may even be seen laughing. He proportions his exertions to his excitements: having been accustomed to converse with deep and lofty thoughts, it is not to be expected that he will flare or sparkle in ordinary chit-chat. One sees no pebbles glittering at the bottom of the Atlantic. U.

———

When we call names, they unluckily are always bad ones. U.

Hard words are much too easy. u.

Les philosophes n'ont fait souvent que changer le vrai en l'équivoque. u.

Les châteaux en Espagne ont perdu beaucoup de gens, même Buonaparte. u.

Every wise man lives in an observatory. u.

The classical universe is a perfect sphere with the earth for its centre: the modern is a multitudinous flood of worlds, the centre of which is the unattainable object of endless research. u.

Selfishness confounds and reverses all relations. Postumous charity is injustice; a mistress is the meanest of slaves.

Some obtain money under false pretences;

some only hearts. Of these two kinds of swindling, it is easy to see which is the most severely punished by law, and perhaps not much harder to find out which is the most offensive.

If there is carrion to feed the crows, there are also crows to feed on carrion.

Amours are fragments of loves; and by heaping one upon another the dissolute expect apparently to make up love at last. But accumulation is not union: a thousand bits of glass are not a mirror: and though a man may have almost every thing else in a seraglio, he cannot have a wife.

Why did not Goethe ever marry?

His mistresses would not let him.

Mistresses! out upon him! How many had he?

Only the nine Muses.

And what business had they to interfere?

Somebody once asked him how the human race would have been propagated, if Adam had not fallen. His answer was: *There can be no doubt: by reasonable discourse.* Perhaps the beginning of the fourth chapter of Genesis was in his mind; and he remembered that carnal knowledge is only the *caput mortuum* of spiritual knowledge. U.

———

A coquette thinks she is worthy to be beloved, and likes to see men become her lovers, not being aware that love is misery, from her own ignorance of the passion. Would you know how to deal with one, who is beginning to jilt you, and encouraging another in the notion that you are secured? Profess an entire devotion: affirm that she is the most.. everything in the world: but do so with a sleepy indifference: if there be anything in the shape of a woman at all pretty in the house, follow her, hunt her, look at her, talk to her; yet tell her and all the world that you do not love her, but are in love with the lady coquette. She and all the world will believe you; but the lady coquette will be alarmed: she will regild her chains, and look to the links. By proper management you will make her so far anxious about you, that it will be your own fault if she does not marry you: and after marriage no English woman is a coquette: no modest woman who exhibits the love of sway, which is the coquetry of modesty, before marriage, will after it affect a dominion over any but her husband. It is hardly possible to excite a strong passion in a heart which admires admiration. But the moment the craving to be universally loved is overcome, (and I believe a husband to be the only *aqua fortis* that eats away the disease), at that moment true love may be begotten, nursed, and educated.   I.

Rien n'est plus petit que le grand monde.

U.

He must have been a preposterous regrater, who first fancied that his brother by preventing hindered him. u.

Falsehood is lying : it implies an utter prostration and downtroddenness of the soul. u.

A drunken man is fitly named : he has drunk, till he is drunken : the wine swallows his consciousness, and it sinks therein. u.

The often noticed superiority of pleasures in anticipation to pleasures in enjoyment, is owing to our unquenchable appetite for spiritual activity. So long as the mind is busy, the pleasure lasts; but when the call for exertion ceases because the object is attained, we begin to flag, and want something new to excite us. So immeasurably are the senses below the soul, even sensual delights hardly gratify except in thought.

"The most voluptuous and loose person breathing, (says South, Vol. i. p. 20.) were he tied to follow his hawks and his hounds, his dice and his courtships every day, would find it the greatest torment and calamity: he would fly to the mines and the gallies for recreation from the misery of unintermitted-pleasure. But there is no action, the usefulness of which has made it the matter of duty and of a profession, but a man may bear the continual pursuit of it, without loathing or satiety. The same shop and trade that employ a man in his youth, employ him also in his age. Every morning he rises fresh to his hammer and his anvil; he passes the day singing; his shop is his element, and he cannot with any enjoyment of himself live out of it." This is to be accounted for from the activity of the mind in the latter case, and from its inactivity in the former. Nothing is less weariable than the soul; nothing more weariable than the body, unless where the soul upholds it. In the would-be man of pleasure (for the title is a false one) all the higher faculties are suspended. Now it is a curse attendant on the blessing of reason, or, to speak more correctly, into which that blessing by abuse may be perverted, that we cannot cast it away from us: we cannot become as if we had never been gifted with it. South contrasts a little before " the stillness of a sow at her wash," with " the silence of an Archimedes in the study of a problem." Man may rise into the latter; he cannot sink into the former. We cannot bring ourselves to walk on all fours: so unless we keep ourselves upright, quadrupeds have the advantage of us and may trample over us as we lie flat on the ground. Conscience must either assist or resist us; and her resistance will disable us for enjoying the stillness of the sow. But the mechanic on the other hand is happy, if so be he is at one with himself; although there is a greater sameness in his occupation, although that occupation, from being less free and from other causes, may seem less amusing: and yet I should not have called it less free; for no lash of slavery is so galling as that which drives the voluptuary to his task-work. The mechanic has a charm against weariness: he sings in his forge or his saw-pit; his conscience tells him he is doing his duty; he indulges perhaps in hopeful visions, visions which that cheering conscience justifies, of a brighter future and an easy old age, when he may sit contentedly before his own hearth; he feels that he is earning the bread of his wife and children, and he looks to the loving welcome which awaits his return. U.

People talk about wearisome sameness: variety is often more wearisome. We tire much sooner of turning over the leaves of a book, than of reading straight onward. Continuous labour often strengthens: dissipation always enervates. Nobody ever felt ennui, until somebody found out that he had nothing to do.   u.

Gaping and yawning are indications of emptiness, at least in inanimate nature.   u.

Attention implies tension or stretch or exertion. You cannot follow, unless you step. Yet most hearers fancy that mere hearing will do; or if they stretch themselves it is to yawn.

                                                               u.

The wise are like the daughters of Danaus, and the ears of mankind are their sieve.   u.

Patience is sufferance, and often hard enough. But nothing great or good can be done without it.   u.

Some minds are made of blotting-paper: you can write nothing on them distinctly. They swallow the ink, and you find a large black spot. U.

Indigestion, they say, is the source of more than half our bodily maladies; and so it is of more than half our mental. Against either the only true medicine is temperance, or σωφροσύνη, as the Greeks rightly called it. U.

Give and forgive. This is nearly the sum of our social duties. U.

Forgiveness is not very difficult, except where there is nothing to forgive. Let this too be difficult to us, or rather let it be impossible. We can easily make it so, by impressing on our hearts that such cases need no forgiveness, nor indeed admit of any; if it be not toward ourselves from the innocent person against whom we have taken offence wrongfully.

Be quick to forgive your neighbour, slow to forgive yourself. U.

A case which needs many words to make it out, like a suit in Chancery, seldom repays. U.

Reasons ought to be causes: often they are only excuses. U.

In writing, as in fencing, what characterizes the beginner is the waste of strength. He strikes much oftener than he hits, and rather flaps his wings than flies on them. The energy put forth may be more than sufficient; but he cannot manage or direct it: some of it runs off to the right hand, more to the left: it proceeds not straightforward to its aim, but digresses into curves and triangles or rather polygons, building one hump on the back of another; and if it ever reach the goal, it has long since flagged and is worn out. There is the fear too of falling short, which sometimes leads to overshooting the mark; the fear of not roasting the bird enough, to avoid which all its juices are burnt out. Then there is the mistake of violence for force, of loudness for emphasis, of words for thoughts; the determination to leave nothing unsaid that one can anywise say, to overload the table, lest there should not be enough to eat, to empty out one's purse before the world, lest they should be ignorant how much it contains. Truly doth Schiller sing:

> Masters in art, lore, science, are known by what they accomplish:
> But it is what he omits, shews me the master in style.

All this is common and natural and easily intelligible. It is somewhat more perplexing at first thought, that young writers should be so fond of looking only at the dark side of things. When one hears talk about the heyday and high spirits of youth, one looks for the reverse. But the scribbling youth are not always the high-spirited. Too often their spirits have burnt to the socket beside their candle as it affronts the dawn: too often they have evaporated during the attempt to condense them into sentences. This led Schiller, whose intercourse was chiefly with such, to exclaim in another epigram:

Has it been always as now? I see but a riddle around me.
Old age only is young, ah! and the young are so old.

Besides there is something irresistibly fascinating, is there not? in the notion of being "grand, gloomy, and peculiar," as some Irishman found out that Buonaparte was, of "sitting a pen-in-hand hermit rapt in the solitude of one's own awful originality." Mirth is vulgar: any cottager can be happy, even though he can neither write nor read: one becomes immeasurably more interesting when one has put on a woe-begone face, when one has none of that ruddiness which the common wind imprints on the cheek by its kisses, and has learnt to look "melancholy and gentleman-like." Far better off still are you, if you can emit certain volumes of smoky sooty misanthropy. Surely he must be a superhuman being, who can discover nothing but wickedness on earth. How can one help loving him, who hates all mankind! Such as remember the commotion excited by the appearance of a late noble poet, will acknowledge the truth of these remarks.

There are other causes however which lie deeper, and are not thus dependent on the silly vanity of individuals. In the first efforts of the mind to grasp the world, or to act upon it, many a hinderance must needs be encountered, many a rebuff must be endured: we must have been fashioned by the discipline of the winds and waves, before we can steer clear of the quicksand or weather the point. Few ever learnt to skate without several tumbles: nor are the light gliding rapid motion of authorship, its graceful steady-balance, its occasional sudden but compact and well-formed figures, of readier acquirement. Is it not natural then that we should quarrel with and abuse what repells us? that, although the failure is our own, we should throw off the fault on something else? He who stumbles or slips, will swear at a stone or a bit of orange-peel: for the last place where people think of laying blame or any other nuisance, is at their own door. The young man has devised for himself a romance of life, and a romance of course must have a hero; but life takes no pains to shape itself after that romance, and the hero turns out not to be one: so life, not being just what he wanted, is worthless and wretched and naught. This error is often difficult to be got over, and some there have been who have never got over it; some who have gone down into the grave, having scarce gleaned one glad moment from their existence. But they who are born to teach mankind, are wiser: they go out into the open harvest-field and reap gladness, the greater part, it may be, for others, but some little assuredly for themselves. It is the jaundiced heart that sees the jaundice in the world: it is the heart at enmity with itself, that looks upon the world as its enemy. Only let the voice of duty be listened to, let her call be obeyed, let her task-work be performed diligently and patiently; and the world will seem to smile on us and to welcome us like a friend: we can hardly fail of loving those toward whom we are conscious of having done our duty.

In intellectual as in active life, the still small voice wherein speaks the true genius, "that peculiar sway of nature which (as Milton saith) also is God's working," will usually be preceded by the strong wind and the earthquake and the fire, which may rend the mountains and break the rocks in pieces, but in which there is nothing that abideth. The poet will at first try force and endeavour to take Beauty by storm; but if he would succeed, he must assure himself that she consents not to be won; until she has been wooed by duteous and loyal service. This appears a simple and easy lesson; yet few among the sons of men have duly apprehended it, except tardily and on compulsion. There may indeed have been others even in modern times, who have felt and known these truths instinctively from their childhood upward; but I cannot name any besides Raphael. Of him it may truly be said that Beauty was his nurse, that he had sucked at her breast, and been dandled in her arms, and had laughed in her eyes, and been covered with her kisses, until all her features were indelibly written on his mind, and her image became amalgamated and, as it were, one with its essence. From his earliest sketch unto his last great work, whatever came from his pencil appears, so to say, to have been steeped in beauty: in his imagination, as in the bright atmosphere of a summer day, every object was arrayed in a loveliness at once its own and his: for all he gives is so genuine and appropriate, it is impossible to distinguish what is native from what is adventitious. But Raphael had the good fortune to be born earlier in the world's great year, when the sun might safely rise without a cloud: in these autumnal times one can hardly hope for a fine day, unless it be ushered in by a misty morning.'

Instead of pursuing these reflexions, let me introduce a passage from a work which I have met with since writing the above. It is so accordant with the whole tenour of the foregoing observations, and of many others scattered through these little volumes, that it has imparted to me the delight which one feels at discovering the thoughts one has laboriously attained to, laid down in their simple evidence by a favorite and honoured author; as if on emerging from a huge pathless forest you were to perceive a loved friend assuring you with a voice sweetened by its kindness that you are in the right way. The passage I speak of is from the remains of Solger, whose early death is among the greatest losses ever sustained by Philosophy: for I know not who among the moderns was ever so well fitted out by nature to do for us, what Plato did for the Greeks. On completing his twentieth year Solger wrote as follows in his Journal:

"I have been for some time in an unpleasant state of mind. I look with ever increasing dislike on the whole life and doings of the present age; and my higher wishes often harass me, because I see their fulfilment is yet far off. How much I longed to become a man who could throw some new light on the ideas of Law and Government, and could unite therewith a more than common familiarity with literature. Toward this end I labour often with great and prosperous zeal, and then I see it again on a sudden so far from me, I see so many difficulties which will hereafter oppose me. But nothing vexes me often more, than the want of literary breeding which I observe in most of my contemporaries, their incapacity of enthusiasm, the inability of most to reach any higher degree of friendship and love. Or are they really better than I think them? Does the cause of this delusion lie in myself, or partly in my present situation?

" These are no motives, says Duty, to shrink away from the path, which thy reason and thy heart prescribe to thee, no grounds for relinquishing that to which thine inward sovereign directs thee. Journey on uninterruptedly along the road thou hast taken; achieve as much as thou canst: with regard to what lies beyond, quiet thyself about it, as reason enjoins. The friendship and love which thou seekest, begin with imparting them thyself; nay, heighten thine inward store of these noble affections, so that, however often thou mayest be turned painfully back, coldness toward thy fellow-creatures may never take possession of thee.

Trust all mankind, and yet never despond if any thrust thee from him.

" O, if I could ever get so far! but thither none perhaps arrives. With me all is still far otherwise: often my vanity is hurt, and I deem my heart injured; often the love of ease is too powerful; often I am too selfish. This too not seldom casts me down. How it will pain me, if a friend is colder, more indifferent toward me! yet without my having done a great deal to make myself pleasing to him; and often more from selfishness and vanity, than because I love him. This must away, altogether away. All my too great dependence on the opinion of others about me, whereof overmuch praise at school has given me a main part, must away. (Let me request the reader to compare the last sentence with what was said in the other volume about the mischief of praise.) Everything must seem to me such as it is. If I give pleasure to others, it must be for the sake of giving them pleasure, not in order that they should thank me for it, or think well of me. I must endeavour to be pleasing unto all, but only on its own account; and then it will not pain me so, if I sometimes find not the gratitude, the esteem, I may have deserved. Disinterestedness, resignation toward mankind, the great word Simplicity, express all that should make me a man." U.

The higher we ascend on the mountain of knowledge, although our horizon may proportionably widen, enabling us to comprehend a greater multitude of objects within it, still we not only perceive that we see much only dimly and confusedly, but we are more and more convinced that a far larger and fairer prospect remains unseen, and that no edifice raised by human hands will ever reach the sky. U.

The tower of Babel could never have been built

in a mountainous country: nature there awes and defies rivalry. u.

It is the business of the human mind to systematize in order that it may atone the complex mass of objects which are subjected to its various perceptions. Every acknowledgement of an ultimate distinction, except that between good and evil (and even this mysterious opposition can hardly be recognized by the Reason without Manicheism, or denied without Pantheism,) every acknowledgement that we cannot perceive how two things, be they what they may, can be reconciled, is an acknowledgement that our faculties are limited and incapable of penetrating to the contemplation of the one all-pervading essence. No single fact or phenomenon can be deemed to have been completely solved, until it has been resolved into its primal elements, until it has been traced up to the point of its emanating from God: so that no one thing will be thoroughly known, until all things are thoroughly known, and Science, far as it may advance, can never be more than the ever approaching asymptote of Truth. u.

Every eye has a dark spot in it. O that all had a light one! u.

Will there be any books in Paradise? If there are, they will be all Gospels. u.

The life of the body is a perpetual metamorphosis: the life of the soul is a perpetual metempsychosis. u.

Every moral teacher is an abolitionist of slavery. u.

The last and fullest theory on any subject enables us better to fix both the positive and the relative value of all previous treatises concerning it. Only after the sun has mounted above the horizon, do we perceive the cause and nature of twilight. From the blossom we can trace the sap down to the root; but we cannot *a priori* from the root educe the blossom. We reason from effects to causes, rather than from causes to effects: for our Reason needs the leading-strings of Experience. There is nothing more amusing, it is true, and little more instructive, than to follow the march of the human mind through any particular region of knowledge: but in such investigations it is well to have the map of the country according to the latest and correctest survey lying open before us, to understand the difficulties which were to be, which have been, and which still remain to be overcome, and then to examine the manner of accomplishing what has already been done. This is far better than creeping at the heels of successive discoverers, borrowing their eye-glasses, and throwing aside the improved telescopes of the present day, through fear of seeing further than they did: for in this way we shall rarely see so far; since few men have ever emptied out all the contents of their minds, at least if there was much in them, on paper, or communicated all their knowledge, still less their power and art of applying it. The civilized man may be better off than the savage, but not as a savage. U.

Apprehension may breed fear: comprehension produces confidence. U.

Invention is only coming upon a thing, and often stumbling over it. U.

An abridgement may be a bridge: it may help us over the water: but it keeps us from drinking. U.

It is impossible for an assiduous reader of

reviews to have a strong and sound mind. They are instruments of intellectual jacobinism, lifting up the low into an atmosphere wherein they cannot breathe, and depressing the high till their mountain spirit loses its tone and elasticity amid the thick fogs of the valley. u.

There is an intellectual and moral and spiritual as well as a political jacobinism: and the former are the more mischievous: indeed without their aid the last would do but little.

Perhaps however it is this very universality of its action, that constitutes the essence of jacobinism, and distinguishes it from all other manifestations of the revolutionary or democratical spirit. Its aim was not to redress immediate practical civil grievances; but to dethrone law, to cast down authority, to strip off custom, to demolish sublimity, to spoil beauty: it blighted the feelings, it stifled the affections, it seared the heart as with a red-hot iron, it drenched the soul in blood.

It was insurgent, rebellious, sensual, demoralizing, brutalizing, atheistical.

Man is the only animal that can do wrong, or right.

It is not until the sun or moon is shining on them from the heavens, that bodies cast strong and well-defined shadows. Similar to this is the effect which has been produced by the rising of Christianity in the moral world. It has marked the outlines of human duties, so that they cannot be mistaken. It has distinguished clearly between the bright and the dark side, between that which looks unto the source of all blessing, and that which turns itself away from it. Reason may indeed give light: but that light is almost as before the light was divided from the darkness: it is without warmth: it is not sunshine. Whereas religion not only enables us to see; it helps us to grow; it ripens and flavours our good deeds; and it produces in us the wholesome conviction that their sweetness, if they should have any, is not of our bestowing, nor comes of the earth, but has descended on them from above, and that all we can do to promote it, is, so to station ourselves as to face and catch the rays. u.

The doctrine of original sin has hardly ever been disputed, except by those whose hearts seemed to tell them that it was a matter of supererogation. u.

Would that sermons oftener contained something besides the *Argumentum ad Hominem*. u.

So prone is our nature to idolatry, many make an idol even of the Bible. Idolatry is the menial slavery to the letter; religion is the willing and reasonable service to the spirit. u.

Some men intend their religion to be a sop for Cerberus. But Cerberus will have too good taste to touch anything so mawkish. *u.*

Emending is removing a fault: to save trouble we have shortened it into mending. It is a stinging joke, and it hits the right place. Menders pick more holes than they darn: instead of patching they botch; and they think they are quite sure of blotting out what is wrong, if they only make the blot big enough. *u.*

When a watch goes ill, it is not enough to move the hands; you must set the regulator. When a man does ill, it is not enough to alter his handiwork, you must regulate his heart. *u.*

All large states have their savages; the richest and most civilized the worst.

In terra decora est iniquitas, in homine fœda.
                                                            U.

Walk into a large town; you will see many crippled bodies. Abide there; you will find the crippled souls outnumber them a hundred to one.   U.

Paris is the city to be abroad in: London is the city to be at home in.   A.

It is to be wished that we could render into English those expressive Greek adjectives in which contrarieties are united, such as θρασύδειλος, γλυκύπικρος. They are so often applicable to the incongruous medleys found in human nature and in social life.   U.

There is a remarkable aptness in the comparison of ancient poetry with Sculpture, and of modern poetry with Painting. The dominion of Painting is larger; her subjects are far more numerous and various; she is more fanciful, and perhaps also more imaginative: that is, she can bring together and combine a greater multitude of objects, can give a vivid expression to a greater throng and complication of feelings, and can array the whole in a gorgeous panoply of colours, like that wherewith the sun invests his satellite worlds as they keep watch around his throne. But the beauty of a statue is perhaps purer, more ideal, more permanent, more absolute, more complete. It is, like the Ptolemaic conception of the universe, finite and comprehensible; while the modern Copernican system is infinite and incomprehensible. Thus in every region of thought we may discover traces of the pervading distinction, so curiously and cunningly exprest by language, that arch keeper and betrayer of secrets: for what we only *understand*, the Greeks ἐπίστανται or *overstand*: our knowledge acknowledges its own inferiority; theirs felt conscious of its mastery: and this was natural; since almost everything with them was of human invention, whereas the original and archetype of all our wisdom is divine. No wonder then that their spirit contemplated itself as overstriding the earth, like the Rhodian Colossus; while ours must look for its symbol to that ancient legend in which Atlas is supporting the heavens.

Again, Sculpture is more satisfactory: it fills the mind more, at least those faculties of the mind which it calls into action. Painting on the other hand, although it may arouse more and even nobler powers, although it may strike a higher, a deeper, and a more varied strain, although it may hoist a greater press of sail, will usually stop short just before reaching the harbour, and leave us either to gaze at the land from the deck, or to swim ashore. After looking at a fine picture, the imagination still hungers for something more; a fine statue is enough in itself: it excites no appetite, but what at the same moment it gratifies. Is there not a somewhat similar contrast between the tragedies of Sophocles and Shakspeare? and are they not both analogous to that between the Grecian temple and the Gothic minster? Is not every Grecian temple complete even though it be in ruins? just as the very fragments of their poems are like the scattered leaves of some unfading flower. Is not every Gothic minster unfinished? and for the best of reasons, because it is infinite. The spirit of the Greeks is always melodious; that of the moderns, when in its prime, is harmonious.

Moreover, the personages in modern poetry act upon us not only by what they themselves are and do and suffer, but also by much that is circumstantial and accidental. The revelation of a common parent has led man to regard Nature with a stronger sympathy, a feeling almost like that of brotherhood. He seeks too and discovers evidence in her, that the sympathy is reciprocal, that the affection is returned. Hence in the vision of the imagination the subhuman accompaniments, whether animate or inanimate, often become as it were a living part of the character. Their meaning is not merely allusive, as in Minerva's owl, or Mercury's caduceus, but implies a closer and more intimate communion. Una is not Una, without her "milkwhite lamb," her "lowly asse more white than snow," her lion that "would not leave her desolate," without the "shady place" in which she "makes a sunshine." The moonlight, the stars, the garden, are mixt up with the image of Juliet. Lear's madness would lose much of its appalling dazzling sublimity, if all the elements had not "with two pernicious daughters joined their high-engendered battles 'gainst a head so old and white." Let any one compare the tone in which Lear calls upon the storm at the beginning of that terrific scene, with the cold majestic defiance of Prometheus at the close of Eschylus's tragedy; and he may readily discern one of the chief distinctions between ancient poetry and modern: for while Lear endues the elemental powers with the feelings and passions of humanity, Prometheus regards them only as the helpless inanimate ministers of Jove; and all the qualities which the poet's epithets assign to them in order to deepen their horror, are drawn solely from their physical appearance. " The earth is shaken; the roaring sound of the thunder bellows; the fiery curls of the lightning flash; the whirlwinds roll the dust; the blasts of all winds leap in adverse faction against each other; the sky is confounded with the sea." Even the metaphor derived from the hostility of opposite factions goes no further than the outward form: there is no design of attributing, what every modern would have attributed, the angry spirit of factions to the winds: Prometheus does not call on them to "rage" and "crack their cheeks." Still less is there anything like " taxing the elements with unkindness:" such a thought could never have occurred except to one who had habitually looked on nature with kindness, and found an answering kindness in her. I may remark too here by the way, since it is intimately connected with this whole discussion, that in Shakspeare even such epithets as are not of the spiritual kind I have been referring to, still are mostly secondary, so to call them, rather than primary: they do not float on the surface, but dive down before they come up again: they go beyond the immediate external appearance, and call for a meditative act of the imagination, by incorporating the effect with the cause. Thus the thunder is not the roaring but the "all-shaking," and the flashes of lightning are the "thought-executing vaunt-couriers to oak-cleaving thunderbolts." This is grand, but it is not classical: for the outlines of the image are nearly lost in the massy folds of the drapery. It would almost seem indeed as if no idea were sufficient for our minds, until it has been placed in communication with a myriad of other ideas: that is to say, our perceptions require to be set a-going by our reflexions. The Greeks on the contrary were so acutely sensitive to the realities of nature, that they needed no such stimulants: the mere sound and sight of a storm were sublime enough for them, even without infusing into it anything like intelligent agency: or rather they transferred the intelligence to human forms, and then seated them on Olympus, instead of amalgaming it as we do with the material objects themselves: their anthropomorphism would seldom allow them to bestow even the particle of a soul on any shape of existence unlike their own. A hurricane is the work of Eolus or Neptune: a pestilence is scattered by the arrows of Apollo: if Etna sends forth her torrents of liquid fire, there is a legend to account for it : " the rage of the imprisoned Typhœus is boiling over in hot bolts of insatiable flame-breathing fury." The conflict too which the ancients conceived themselves to be evermore waging with fate, and the irrepressible consciousness of their own superiority, at least of the superiority of their conceptions and ideas, to anything they had been taught to venerate as divine, induced them to insulate themselves from the world, and to aim at existing, statue-like, independent of circumstances, or even to trample on them. Hence, although we are wont to take our tone from time and place, they chose rather to know nothing of them. Helen, and Achilles, and Antigone, and Ajax, and Edipus, are nowhere or anywhere : they belong to no place; that is, they may exist in any place ; for that which is around them is no part of them, and may be removed, except so far as it is the necessary means of their action : there is nothing about them merely accessary and ornamental; nothing but what penetrates immediately to the core of their humanity; like the urn in which Electra conceives she is holding the ashes of her brother. In other words they are like figures of sculpture: for it is one among the prerogatives of sculpture to emancipate its subjects, so far as may be, from time and space, "the bonds of our humanity," and to exhibit them in the fullness and freedom of an almost ideal existence. A statue knows nothing of *where* or *when*: it is of no fixed place, of no definite time; it is in the eye, and in the mind, and passes almost like a thought from the sculptor to the beholder.

Here I must recur for a moment to a topic already alluded to, the indefiniteness and dimness and dreaminess of modern poetry, its ceaseless intermingling and unweariable accumulation of colours, hue running into and overrunning hue, its perpetual striving to go out of the subject and beyond it, and to seize everything which can in any way be hooked on it, the hundred arms which it stretches out like one of the Titans to grasp whatever comes within its reach. All this, it is evident, can nowise be reconciled with the substantial distinctly limited form, and gentle, almost passionless and spiritualized, reality of Sculpture. Nor can Painting at all keep up with Poetry in such things; but she can follow in her train.

Besides a statue may not be fanciful; nay its character is rather ideal than imaginative. Sculpture can hardly attempt any thing like a new combination of forms: it must confine itself almost entirely to such as actually exist, and among these will apply itself most diligently to the human, as the noblest, the most beautiful, the most majestic, the most intellectual: indeed the mere absence of any fur or other covering from the skin would of itself be nearly enough to determine the preference. Now the poetry of the Greeks was likewise almost exclusively human. Animal poetry and animal sculpture, have long flourished in the East, where the quadruped has not seldom been a nobler, and sometimes a more rational, creature than the biped. But although one perceives certain traces of something like fellowship with animals in Homer, in the horses of Achilles, the dog Argus, and the pathetic complaint of Polyphemus to his ram, the later Greeks soon turned them out of their thoughts, as is natural in the progress of civilization : so natural indeed, that, had we no other reasons for being grateful to chivalry, we should still owe it our best thanks for having led us to keep friends with the horse.

A statue then must not depart too far from reality : it may represent a faun or a satyr, a centaur or a mermaid : for in these combinations the animal part is headed and over-ruled by the human. Perhaps too it may have been Sculpture that gave rise to some of these combinations; since the graceful forms of an animal's body become a worthier subject for the chisel, when a human head is placed upon it. But fairies and goblins and witches and ghosts and spectres, the whole offspring of modern imagination, must be left to Painting.

For the subject of Sculpture should in some degree possess beauty of form. It must have something which wooes us to permanency of contemplation, something which may justify its being thus perpetuated. The dramatic masks, which were often hideous enough, were made to serve temporary and subordinate purposes. From these reasons I am unable to conceive a statue of Satan. Mr. Chantrey indeed is said to be engaged about one: but I feel almost convinced that his enterprise is grounded on a mistake. What he will try to embody, will probably be the bastard Satan of Paradise Lost, not the genuine one of the old Christian mythology: and yet even here he can hardly be successful. He may bring forth an ingenious, or even a fine work: but it will not be comparable even to his own statue of Watt: it will convey a very faint conception of the Spirit of Evil. If he tries to fix and petrify the features in any mask of demoniacal expression, his failure is certain. Not to speak of the whiteness so repugnant to our notions, the very solidity and bright purity of marble resist his undertaking: they as it were appropriate Sculpture to the portraiture of what is enduring. But evil by its very essence is transitory and perishable above every thing: it subsists only by perpetually destroying not only all else, but itself: it is a Chaos without form and void, because the spirit of God doth not move upon its face. Τὸ γὰρ κακὸν τοῦ ἀπείρου, ὡς οἱ Πυθαγόρειοι εἴκαζον· τὸ δὲ ἀγαθὸν τοῦ πεπερασμένου. *Aristot. Ethic.* II. 5.

Durability then is another condition in a subject well adapted for sculpture; which unfits it for representing either the agonies of bodily suffering, or the trance of any violent and therefore momentary passion. I know, the Laocoon may be objected to me: but that extraoidinary work belongs to an age when the art had already passed its maturity, and was declining. At such a time a clever man goes too readily astray after any glimmering of a meteor-like novelty, and will try anything, provided it be different from what his predecessors have accomplished. Even that monstrous extravagance in the dome of Milan, the statue of the saint who has just been flayed, finds admirers, and is almost as ingenious as it is disgusting. Nor was the artist of the Laocoon unaware what a reluctant theme he had to contend with, or ignorant of the restrictions imposed on him by the peculiar nature of his art. So far as his subject would allow, he has conformed to them. Winkelmann has noticed this in his celebrated description of that statue: "As the depth of the sea (he says) always continues tranquil, however the surface may rage, so the expression in the Greek statues shews amid all the passions a calm and stedfast soul. This soul displays itself in the face of the Laocoon, and not in his face alone, together with the most violent suffering. The pain exhibited by every muscle and nerve of the body, and which, without looking at the face and other parts, one seems almost to feel oneself, in the convulsive contraction of the loins; this pain does not vent itself with any violence in the face or the attitude. He lifts up no terrible scream, as Virgil sings of his Laocoon. The opening of the mouth does not allow this: it is rather a stifled sigh of agony, a *gemitus ingens*, as Sadoletus describes it. The suffering of the body and the strength of the soul are distributed with equal force through the whole structure of the figure, and as it were balanced. His misery pierces to our heart; but we wish that we could endure misery as bravely as this great man." Like Cesar in his hour of death, he folds the mantle of seemliness around his agonies, and is studious to die as became the priest of Apollo. Thus the Laocoon rather confirms than refutes what has been said. It is, like *Paradise Lost,* I will not say a splendid error, but a splendid anomaly; and great as are the talents it displays, it is to be passed by with a mere side-view, when one is laying down the canon of statuary, even as *Paradise Lost* must, when one is laying down the canon of epic poetry. How different from this Laocoon is the Ugolino such as one sometimes sees him, weak, emaciated, haggard, grinning, tearing his hair, gnashing his teeth! in the Laocoon the soul rises above and quiets the troubled body; in the Ugolino the soul itself is the centre of the strife. That the tragedy of the Athenians was regulated by similar principles, one may perceive in the studious removal of everything atrocious from sight: no deed was to be perpetrated on the stage, no situation was to be exhibited, which it would have misbecome a statuary to express.

Nor on the other hand is Sculpture much better adapted for representing the sacred personages of our religion. True, Michel Angelo, for whose genius no effort was too arduous, sometimes attempted it; and Dannecker is reported to have surpassed all that was deemed possible, in the cast for his statue of Christ. But the disuse of Sculpture in modern times, except for the portraiture of individuals, is of itself the best evidence of its unsuitableness to our ways of thinking: even as the employment of Painting among the ancients chiefly on subjects of a lower and less momentous kind, proves that it was not the right exponent for their ideas. Such things indeed may seem to be determined by chance; which however can determine nothing, seeing that it is nothing but a logical symbol for an unknown power, hour of death, he folds the mantle of seemliness around his agonies, and is studious to die as became the priest of Apollo. Thus the Laocoon rather confirms than refutes what has been said. It is, like *Paradise Lost*, I will not say a splendid error, but a splendid anomaly; and great as are the talents it displays, it is to be passed by with a mere side-view, when one is laying down the canon of statuary, even as *Paradise Lost* must, when one is laying down the canon of epic poetry. How different from this Laocoon is the Ugolino such as one sometimes sees him, weak, emaciated, haggard, grinning, tearing his hair, gnashing his teeth! in the Laocoon the soul rises above and quiets the troubled body; in the Ugolino the soul itself is the centre of the strife. That the tragedy of the Athenians was regulated by similar principles, one may perceive in the studious removal of everything atrocious from sight: no deed was to be perpetrated on the stage, no situation was to be exhibited, which it would have misbecome a statuary to express.

Nor on the other hand is Sculpture much better adapted for representing the sacred personages of our religion. True, Michel Angelo, for whose genius no effort was too arduous, sometimes attempted it; and Dannecker is reported to have surpassed all that was deemed possible, in the cast for his statue of Christ. But the disuse of Sculpture in modern times, except for the portraiture of individuals, is of itself the best evidence of its unsuitableness to our ways of thinking: even as the employment of Painting among the ancients chiefly on subjects of a lower and less momentous kind, proves that it was not the right exponent for their ideas. Such things indeed may seem to be determined by chance; which however can determine nothing, seeing that it is nothing but a logical symbol for an unknown power, corresponding to the x and y of the algebraist: they may seem to be determined by a blind unreasoning instinct; but that instinct has a marvellous faculty for scenting out what is right and fitting; nor can any axiom be safer, than that, where there is any such general effect, there must have been a good and efficient cause for it. And after all the very best statue of Jesus or of his Mother must be greatly inadequate; not merely from the insufficiency of all art, but from causes peculiar to Sculpture, the impediments of which do not incumber Painting. Our Saviour and the Virgin Mary are always surrounded by a halo of vivid feeling: they are not wrapt up in themselves, as the Deities of the Pagans were, that, like statues,

> Immortali ævo summa cum pace fruuntur,
> Semota ab nostris rebus, sejunctaque longe......
> Et placidum degunt ævum multumque serenum:

they repose not in the abstracted indifference of self-sufficient beauty: their whole being was sympathy and kindness and benevolence and love. The Mother, as an object of poetical contemplation, lives only in her child; and her heart and her face are full of him, even before his birth: the Saviour lives only in a gracious and mysterious communion with the race he is come to save. All this is inexpressible in sculpture: but in painting there is something visionary, and to all appearance instantaneous and evanescent, which fits it to exhibit the more delicate and fleeting shades of feeling: it looks like a birth of the moment, which one sweep of the brush has brought forth, and which another stroke with the same ease might transform or eraze. For colours are the creatures of light, the most fleeting and mutable of all things. Hence although Sculpture may figure to us the everlasting sorrows of Niobe, of her whom Electra deems a goddess, because "in her rocky tomb she ever weepeth" (*Sophocl. Elect.* 150,); the artist here only realizing what her grief was fabled to have effected; yet even the anguish of the childless Madonna is unwilling to be thus eternized; for the Christian mourner " shall be comforted."

Another blessed reason of the conformity between painting and modern poetry, is the more domestic character of modern life. The bonds of family and kindred are stronger and more indissoluble among Christians than among the Greeks; or at least they ought to be, and therefore imaginatively they are so. The Greeks duly reverenced indeed the duties of kindred; and the pure heavenly spirit of Sophocles, anticipating the feelings of a more favoured age, almost saw that these duties were among our most glorious privileges: still the voice of affection was but dimly heard, and the identity of Wisdom and Love was hardly guessed at: for not yet had the high priest appeared who was to celebrate the holy marriage between the heart and the head. We have grown more social and domestic, even as we are become less civic : as the ties which united us to the state, slackened, we drew nearer and closer to our homes. This might help me to account for the predominance of the social novel above every kind of poetical composition in our days, as well as for its almost total absence, among the ancients. But such a digression would lead me too far astray: suffice it to remark that the characters in modern poetry, as in modern life, stand more togethe than of old. He who comes forward on the stage of public action, is still alone, even in the midst of a mob : Phocion when haranguing the Athenian forum, was as solitary as a ship on the stormy Atlantic, and in that posture might be a subject for a statuary. But when he walked to prison, surrounded by his friends, and with a countenance, as Plutarch describes it, οἷον ὅτε στρατηγῶν ἀπ' ἐκκλησίας προυπέμπετο, both his look and his companions would need a painter to delineate them. For it is with difficulty that Sculpture can represent a groupe: even on a frieze it can hardly do more than repeat somewhat similar figures, as in a procession, or in the battle between the Lapithæ and the Centaurs. This difficulty lies not only in the cumbrousness of the material, in its incompatibility with anything like perspective, and in the determination of every figure to thrust itself in front, where there can be no background, but also in the unfitness of marble noticed above for indicating occasional feeling. It gives only the form, which exhibits the permanent character: but it cannot give the tints of passing emotion, the blush or the paleness of passion. Now where a number of human beings are brought together in such way as to constitute a poetical whole, there must be some one common feeling to reconcile them; and such a feeling cannot be durable, when the instability of every heart is increased by the instability of its neighbour; as in a house of cards every card shakes of itself, and more and more from the contagious shaking of all the others. I have said, Phocion speaking in the forum would be a subject for a statuary; and yet Paul preaching would not: at least Raphael has shewn that the latter argument is far more suitable to the canvas. For the speaker may be severed from his audience more easily than the preacher; political topics, however important, are lifeless and uninteresting in comparison with the welfare of souls; and although the orator may allowably declaim in solitude, there is something revolting in the thought of sacred truths uttered where there is none to hear them; so revolting indeed that, in cases where there were no human auditors, the legends tell us beasts and fishes came to listen.

Still the physical beauty of a statue is more perfect, and more real. This may be substantiated by the evidence of facts, if that be of weight in such discussions. I know not of any one who ever conceived an actual serious passion for a picture: but the story of Pygmalion—for which there was probably some foundation of this sort; and if there was not, no matter: it still shews the belief of those who devised it— those of the French soldier who fell in love with, if I mistake not, the Venus de Medicis, and of the "maid of France" who died for love of the Belvidere Apollo, are well known: and several others might be added. Indeed I once some years ago detected myself kissing the hand of a Venus; but no such attempt to give vent to it ever interrupted my admiration of a picture. And yet on the contrary, when art has been debased for the sake of pampering the licentiousness of diseased imaginations, art which ought to be the organ of all purity and loveliness and majesty, the embodier of every lofty idea, and the peculiar office of which is to manifest the beauty of holiness, those who have thus defiled it, beginning with Parrhasius, have been painters much oftener than sculptors. The cold chastity of marble is not easily to be sullied: hardly can it be brought to provoke anything like sensual intoxication. What might allure, when united with the tints of youth, becomes loathsome and ghastly on the pale cheek of a statue; and the same reasons which unfit sculpture for representing Satan, unfit it almost equally for his crew, and indeed for the whole mystery of iniquity.

The greater part of these remarks might be illustrated by reference to the corresponding features in ancient and modern poetry. Let a single one suffice. The personages in Grecian poetry have a more definite reality; a visible, bodily, as it were statuesque personality*: we see them more palpably before us: they stand out more: we see Helen walking along the walls of Troy; we see Penelope standing at the door of her hall,

Αντα παρειάων σχομένην λιπαρά κρήδεμνα.

we see Achilles standing at the trench, and hear his terrific shout: we see Electra before the tomb of her father: we see Edipus sitting beside the grove of the Eumenides: we see Apollo driving the Furies from his temple: we see them in the lines of the poet, almost as distinctly as we could have seen them on the stage; unmarked indeed by any lesser peculiarities of feature or expression—such things were not generic enough for classical taste—but like statues or figures on reliefs or on vases, graceful, stately, beautiful, in the calm of subdued feeling, in the subsidence of passion, in the majesty of indignant power. Nor is this brought about by means of any elaborate description: the motion of the Greeks was too steady, their hand too firm, for them to need incumbering their imagination with such a drag: they could not perpetrate such a contradiction in terms as descriptive creation. Indeed description, where it is merely descriptive, is essentially unpoetical and unimaginative: for the imagination proceeds not by the aggregation of parts, but by the comprehension of wholes: to be imaginative then, a description must in some measure animate and impersonate, or at least unify, what it describes. Some beautiful specimens of this kind have been produced of late years: we should be careful however lest, as seems not unlikely, the field of poetry be entirely overgrown by description, lest the whole picture be swallowed up by the frame, which is rapidly encroaching upon it. The Greeks, since, as was before remarked, they had not the same spiritual ideas of Nature, were less liable to be diverted from the great object of all poetry, humanity in all its modifications. "Some minds (says Schelling) think about things; others think the things themselves:" a momentous distinction. It is evident that all mere description belongs to the former class: in the latter most of the front places are occupied by the Greeks. Their mode of exhibiting a poetical object, was not by piling detail on detail until the reader sank under the wearisome burthen, but by stripping it of every thing cumbersome and extraneous, by opening out the view full upon it, and by presenting it in action, the most immediate emanation from personality, and its distinctest and least fallible expression. There is something so congenial to her nature in action, that wherever the Imagination discerns it, she runs forward to hail and welcome it. Only shew characters in action, and she will readily supply every thing you do not shew: now action is the outward form and body and, so to say, the statue of character: it displays the broad outlines of character, its piers and buttresses, but not its more delicate tracery. The aim of the moderns on the contrary has been to shew the latter, and not seldom to the great detriment of the former: we exhibit the invisible, we utter the silent, we fix the fugitive, we perpetuate the momentary: not content with seeing the image in the mirror, like the monkey we crawl slyly up and look behind, to find out its original. This however is our aberration and absurdity: what is great amongst us, is truly great; but its greatness differs in kind from that of the Greeks. Nothing can exceed the spiritual reality of Shakspeare's characters; but they have not the same tangible bodily reality I have been speaking of: we know their minds, their hearts, their feelings, their passions, all that is past of their lives, and all that is to come; we know everything about them, except their bodily form. When we try to conceive Hamlet, it is his spirit we see, more spectral than the ghost of his father; when we try to conceive Juliet, we see her love. They may be painted: they cannot be sculptured. Or can any one frame in his mind a statue of Macbeth, or of Othello, or of Lear, or of Falstaff, or of Caliban, or of Don Quixote, or of

Faust, or of Mephistophiles? Yet the pencil has already done much for some of them, and may find an interminable field in the remainder and their comrades. In a word, the ancients may be said to have painted with light, while the moderns dip their brushes into the multitudinous ocean of the clouds, with all their endless pageantry of colours: this may be said, if not generally, at least of their representatives Sophocles and Shakspeare. u.

Most modern writers appear in their dressing-gowns, sometimes even without having pulled off their nightcaps. The Greeks, when they were not naked, wore their tunics girt tightly around them: the Roman seldom laid aside his toga. Eastern poetry on the other hand is so immersed in drapery, in muslins and silks and India shawls and Turkey carpets, with a turban upon it and an ottoman under it, so studious is it to conceal nature, that hardly a morsel of genuine flesh is to be seen; and as for shape, it "has none distinguishable in member, joint, or limb." υ.

The peculiar merit of Roman literature is its urbanity, that refined, dignified, and almost magnanimous good-breeding, which belonged to a city, the mistress of the civilized world. The Athenian ἀστειότης was something very different: it wants the aristocratical grace of the other: it is more trivial, more jocose, and neither claims respect, nor yields it. υ.

Cicero and Horace were gentlemen: the younger Pliny and Martial were courtiers. They no longer breathed the fresh air of freedom, which is as the breath of life to the former character. That character will exist nowhere, except where the rights of the subject are no less sacred than those of the sovereign. If it be rare in any part of the European continent, one of the main reasons will be found to lie in the want of such sacred rights. If it was common under the old monarchy of France, it was among those who lived on their estates, and whose spirits were not bound and worn by the moral fetters of the capital. For if a gentleman is to grow up, he must grow like a tree: there must be nothing between him and heaven.

A friend who was looking over my proof sheets, has just reminded me that Mr. Coleridge in his *Biographia Literaria* (Vol. II. p. 208), when defining the gentlemanly character, has made almost the same remarks as the preceding; only what he says is much more subtile, more accurate, and more complete. To him then whatever is good in them belongs: for I read his observations some ten years ago, and the thought has dwelt within me, although I remembered not whence it came. Perhaps this will have been the case often; so frequently have I strengthened my mind with the invigorating waters which stream forth redundantly in Mr. Coleridge's works, that, if I mistake not, many of my thoughts will appear to have been impregnated by his spirit. If they do, may they not shame their parentage! υ.

Pray be condescending; if for no worthier reason, at least because none can condescend except from higher ground. υ.

Is bread the better for kneading? so is the heart. Knead it then by spiritual exercises; or God must knead it by afflictions.

It is a flagrant blunder, to think of making people good, by making them bad. υ.

Il faut reculer pour mieux sauter; quelquefois peutêtre même dans la morale. Pourtant c'est une vilaine amitié de repousser dans la fosse celui qui veut monter sur les remparts. υ.

Hardships harden the body, and often make the heart gentle. Luxury softens the body, and hardens the heart. U.

Society is the most merciless of conquerors. It wants to fire off its members for its own purposes, and is therefore glad to load them with gunpowder. They often burst indeed: but no matter: more are always to be had. U.

The principle of the ancients was Patriotism, or devotion to the state; that of the moderns is Honour, or reverence for the individual. In the republics of Greece and Rome, where all distinctive peculiarities were absorbed into the national unity, and the glimmering starlight of individual consciousness was put out by the daylight of national consciousness, Honour could hardly have being: no virtues were upheld, but such as were immediately beneficial, no vices were reprobated, but such as were mischievous to the commonwealth. The same train of causes which made the ancients less sensible of the domestic affections, except so far as they were a sacred instinct of Nature which could not be disregarded without impiety, likewise hindered the birth of Honour amongst them: for Honour rising out of the union of all those affections, and impregnated with their sweetest exhalations, is at once the crown that consummates and the sword that protects them. Whatever was imperative on the ancients, was a duty: there were few decencies of life: the Graces, so powerful in the sensuous and intellectual world, stopped short on the frontier of the spiritual: there were no charities. Where the man, as contradistinguished from the citizen, scarcely existed, it must be in vain to look for Honour, that choicest, most essential essence of our purest and loftiest humanity. But Christianity has everywhere revealed duties within duties, duties as it were of a higher power, or, so to say, the fluents of duties, and thereby has enabled us to acquire a deeper insight into the principles of our moral nature. The dealings of Honour are with that which is purely ideal, with that which a coarser analysis is unable to calculate, and which the rude hand of human legislation cannot grasp. In its proper meaning Honour is an application of the great Christian maxim, the uses of which are as unfathomable as the Wisdom and as inexhaustible as the Love it sprang from, to the realities of the affections spiritualized by the imaginative reason; it imposes upon itself all the same observances which it exacts from others; but it likewise exacts from others the same observances which it imposes upon itself. A man may forgive the injuries done to himself, much more readily than the injuries done to his Honour: for his Honour is his higher self, unto which he must not hesitate about sacrificing his earthly life. Honour knows that " whosoever shall keep the whole law, and yet offend in one point, is guilty of all;" and therefore is it so scrupulous about what the vulgar call trifles, "greatly finding quarrels in a straw," so fearful lest the slightest speck should sully the pure white of its raiment. Honour knows that courage is the condition of its own manifestation, and even of its being; it knows too that falsehood is spiritual cowardice: therefore is it so jealously tenacious of courage and of truth. Honour has enlarged the sphere of our personal consciousness, until it embraces all those who are nearest and dearest to us, and feels a wrong done to a wife or sister or mother or daughter no less poignantly, nay far more poignantly, than if it were done to ourselves; above all if it be a wrong done to their souls, an outrage against their moral nature, on the innocence and purity of which we repose with a whole and wholesome faith, at the same time that we may perhaps acknowledge its weakness, and the consequent necessity of defending it against the spoiler. In fine, honour has made it the glorious duty of manhood to protect all those who need protection. υ.

Few institutions of our times, I am disposed to believe, have been more mischievous than the multiplication of honours. Honours often dishonour men. We have even seen that monstrous parody, a Legion of Honour: he whose name is Legion, has seized and endeavoured to appropriate that which can only exist in simplicity and singleness. People are become so crippled and imbecile, that we fancy nobody will ever be able to move, unless we place a crutch of vanity under him. Yet most truly may they who trust in vanity, be said to trust in the staff of a broken reed, whereon if a man lean, it will go into his hand and pierce it. A child cannot do its duty, without being medalled; a soldier cannot do his duty, without being medalled; an officer cannot do his duty, without being ribbanded. And what will, what must be the consequence? that no one will ever think of doing his duty, except for the sake of what he is to get by it. Indeed it will cease to be deemed a duty: the word itself will be an idle incumbrance: our actions will be mere matters of barter, to be balanced against the reward that is offered for them. Honour used to be the military principle; honours are now become the military motives: and as motives, from their coarse gross clumsy nature, have a trick of overlaying principles; so honours are likely to stifle honour; even as reasons often stifle reason, even as candlelight drives moonlight out of the window.

Perhaps however people fancy that they have scriptural authority, and are " provoking one another to good works." If so, let them search the Bible, and see whether that will bear them out. U.

"*Madame, tout est perdu, fors l'honneur*, was the noble letter of Francis the First to his mother after the battle of Pavia. One cannot conceive Buonaparte writing such a letter, except as a mimic. His heart had not struck root deep enough in ancestral feelings: it was not sufficiently upheld by the consciousness of moral dignity: he had no sympathies with the world, and he was therefore aware that the world had no sympathies with him. He knew not even what Honour was. The feeling, if he ever possessed it, had been crushed by the weight of honours with which he had loaded it. Indeed nothing is more remarkable than the prodigious meanness of his soul, in spite of all his prodigious talents. He had no faith in himself, none in mankind, none in God, none of that magnanimous reliance on posterity, wherewith great men have comforted themselves when fortune has set her face against them. His soul was empty as the heart of a volcano: whatever it once contained had been vomited forth, to spread desolation over the world; and nothing at last was to be seen within him, but the smouldering flames of his unappeasable passions. Wordsworth in his pamphlet on the Convention of Cintra prophetically compared the French Emperor's military power "to a huge pine-forest, the ability of which to resist the storm is in its skirts: let but the blast once make an inroad, and it levels the forest and sweeps it away at pleasure." His intellectual power was of a similar nature: gigantic in semblance, wielding a terrific weapon, clad in glittering pitiless steel, like some of the monsters in romance, when once it had been overthrown, it was found to be a heap of bodiless armour.

Landor has justly remarked that he was "an imitator," and as such could have "nothing stable." (*Imag. Conv.* Vol. i. p. 354.) When he fell into the hands of the English, it was in this way he tried to invest his situation with a majesty which he felt did not belong to it. He could not say or do anything great himself; but he could ape the great words or deeds of others. He probably said to the captain of the ship that brought him from Egypt or from Elba: *Cæsarem et fortunam vehis*; and one might wager that he must have said to Talma, or Laplace, perhaps to both: *If I were not Napoleon, I should wish to be Talma, or Laplace.* Neither of these speeches would have been more out of season than his letter to the Prince Regent, in which he compares himself to Themistocles on the hearth of Admetus. One thing at least I am quite sure of: Themistocles, were the scene to come over again, would not compare himself to Buonaparte on board the Bellerophon. The course he adopted, was that of a man who was in earnest, and knew what motives influence his fellow-creatures. He took the boy of Admetus in his arms, he sat on the hearth, actions of a religious significance, which it would have been sacrilege to despise: he appealed to his generosity; he also appealed to his justice: he set forth convincingly the extreme disproportion between any injuries Admetus had received, and the revenging them by giving up a suppliant to those who were seeking his life. If Admetus had betrayed Themistocles, he would have been ungenerous, cruel, unjust, impious. There was some cogency in such arguments. The Greek did not think of settling the matter by an empty swollen phrase, whereby had any been imposed upon, he himself must have caught up the universal jeer, and prolonged it in his sleeve. U.

The best defence is not to give offence:
The only panoply is innocence. U.

Would you see the state of good men under calamity? Look at the sea in a storm. The winds drive and toss its waves: but they cannot harm them: and at length the turmoil is stilled, the light shines on thém from heaven, and the sunbeams sleep or play on the quiet bosom of the waters. u.

Many persons spend their lives in parrying death. But he who would be always on his guard, must sometimes be off his guard. u.

Every body has his own Zenith and Nadir, his own Heaven, and his own Hell. u.

Practical life teaches us that people may differ and that both may be wrong: it also teaches us that people may differ and both be right. Anchor yourself fast in the latter faith, or the former will sweep your heart away. u.

There are men whom you will never dislodge from an opinion, except by taking possession of it yourself. u.

Pourquoi es-tu libertin?

Par politesse.

Pourquoi dépenser tout ton argent?

Par politesse.

Pourquoi dire tant de mensonges?

Mais, par politesse.

Pourquoi vas-tu droit au diable?

Que demandez-vous? Par politesse. Il est si poli, on ne peut lui refuser rien.   U.

Materialism is a circumference without a centre. Idealism is a centre without a circumference.   U.

Scholars have a dreadful dread of making false quantities: I wish philosophers had. But the former blunder is of such paramount importance, that many would feel more ashamed of shortening the penultima of *vectigal*, as Burke did in one of his speeches, than of shortening the returns they send in to the taxgatherer. U.

The Bible is the hardest book I know; and the easiest.

"A paradox (says Frederic Schlegel) is a great truth." Be it so: but at all events it is often a truth on stilts, a truth which, like the sun in Haydn's *Creation,* gives a loud knock at the door to announce its rising. It may be necessary or expedient in particular cases to arouse people from the torpid lethargic sleep of habit or indifference by shaking them somewhat roughly: but this is not the way in which the "gentle touch of morning light" usually awakens us; nor is walking on stilts very suitable to the grace and fair proportions of Truth.

A truism on the other hand is a truth on all fours, or sprawling on the ground and unable to lift itself up.   U.

No work of nature is ever new: no work of man is ever young. Both become old: because man's works, after they have been let out of his hands, are in some measure subjected to the operation of Nature, and are hereby assimilated to her productions, so far at least as to excite a kindred feeling in the beholder. In course of time too, unless man rudely thrust her back, Nature will so blend and intermingle her workmanship with his, that, as in Tintern or Netley Abbey, it is scarcely possible to distinguish the living tracery from the inanimate. But nobody ever called a tree or a bird new, that is, in itself, and with reference to its age: it is only relatively to man that in such things novelty can be predicated, of a species when considered as an object of human knowledge, or of an individual as an object of human possession: for your new horse is not new in itself, but only newly become yours; and the new shells that have been found in the Paris basin, are all antediluvian, if not preadamite. Nobody on the other hand ever talked of a young table, or a young cap : for youth implies a native inherent genuine bloomingness, whereas novelty merely dizens the surface with an artificial momentary gloss. This perhaps is the reason why, although I can love and admire youth, and can love and reverence old age, I always feel a repugnance to novelty and newness. What can be more uncomfortable than a new coat, a new hat, a new pair of shoes? for comfortableness is an attribute which must be acquired, and which no manufacturer can give. I dare not speak about a new gown: the wearer often seems pleased enough with it, much oftener indeed than she seems at home in it. Yet this after all is the real secret of comfort: nothing is comfortable except what one feels at home in. So that if the French actually know not what comfort is, this must arise from a still more wretched deficiency, from their not knowing what it is to be at home. It may be so in the capital: when an Englishman once told Humboldt he was going home, that great explorer of hidden regions asked inquisitively: *Where can that be? there is no such place in all Paris.* Neither is there such a word in the language: it is a blessed Teutonic word. Yet I will not readily believe that this defect, and the other defects, or, as the world calls them, merits, of the metropolis pervade the provinces. Woe to that country in which the Vestal fire is extinct!

A new house again: nothing can be barer or balder or barrener. The Imagination can find nothing in it to cleave to, nothing to look back upon; and it is the nature of the Imagination to be retrospective much rather than prospective: her gaze is evermore cast backward and lingers fondly amid the relics of the past; which the Greeks expressed so beautifully by calling the Muses the daughters of Memory. In a new house there are no associations, no recollections, no traditions, no stories, except the first, second, and third. Nobody has ever been in it, besides the masons and the carpenters and the upholsterers, and other such persons who are known by what they make, not by what they are. But an old house, even when it is not especially endeared to us by having been the abode of our own ancestors, is still richly stored with all the choicest furniture of the Imagination. It has witnessed and been familiar with every human feeling: Birth has gladdened it; Life with all its changeful apparitions has animated it; Death has saddened and consecrated it. Here a mother has sat rejoicing to feel the stream of life passing from her into her infant: here she heard her child lisp its first prayer, or answered its first tremulous question of innocent perplexity about heaven, and patiently tried to make the life she had given more precious, by making it the prelude of a blessed immortality. There children have played, and angered and caressed one another, and trained up their minds amid their little mimic world. Here lovers have talked through the fleeting day, listening to the music of each other's voice, or have first cast down the eyes which had hitherto met so gladly and so frankly, and have turned them inward and seen their own hearts, and have at length told each other what they found there. But it were endless to go through all the incidents which as it were humanize a building, after men have been born and died in it.

The worst thing of all is a new church. I love to say my prayers in a place where my fathers and forefathers have prayed. It may be idleness and vanity to think so, but somehow God seems to be nearer in a building where he has long been more immediately present. There is an odour of sanctity breathing about an old church: the worn stones are hallowed by the feet which have trod and the knees which have knelt on them: so much in it has been changed by Time, that it is become more like a house not made with hands: no body now living can make anything like it; its architect is forgotten; it is the work not of a man but of an age. A new church on the contrary was built by such a man, fitted up by such another: everything about it is so neat and so modern; it is almost as smart as a theatre: there was no such thing five years ago, and what has been so shortlived can never seem to have any permanent reason for its existence, or indeed to have anything permanent about it; and instead of the odour of sanctity, one finds only the smell of paint. It has no atmosphere of prayer: it is not a treasure-house of the dead. My feelings on this subject I should have conceived would have been almost universal, had not an American gentleman once expressed to me his surprise that we let our churches in England, especially the cathedrals, grow so old and dirty. He had seen the minsters of York and Lincoln, and assured me that, if they stood in America, the outside of them would be white-washed every ten years; such being the American way of shewing their reverence for the house of God. How far his statement is correct, I know not. A nation of yesterday may perhaps be destitute of sympathy with the day before: but we in England, I trust, should as soon think of white-washing Helvellyn.

Then there are new books: people are for ever asking you to recommend them some new publication. I would sooner ask a man to recommend me some new wine. If wine improves by keeping, much more do books. A work composed two or three or twenty centuries since, carries me before a different scene of human life; and even if its worth were not greater, its value would be: for it teaches me something which I knew not; whereas most modern works tell you very little, but what from your own experience you know much better already: that is to say, the works of poetry and philosophy, which are conversant with the substance and spirit of things, and which are scarcely, if at all, progressive: for in science, which deals with the shell and carcase, the latest treatise is likely enough to contain the most correct information: even as our roads and our pigstyes may probably be better than those of our ancestors, although in what appertains to architectural beauty or grandeur they are so incomparably our masters. Besides it is wholesome and invigorating to get into a new region of thought, to travel among foreign ideas, and to remark and compare their peculiarities: such a change is no less salutary to the mind, than change of air is to the body: it arouses us from the drowsy torpour of custom; it instructs us more reasonably to appreciate all the circumstances of our being, and to distinguish between new-fangled conventional notions, and principles which are pervading and enduring. Moreover a work will commonly require time to ascend into the sky and take its seat and be established in the firmament, before we can look up at it as bright and everlasting. When once there indeed, it becomes like the rest: all the stars seem to be equidistant from the beholder; and it is not otherwise with the great works of man's intelligence. The star of which the rays have been thousands of years travelling earthward, appears, if we see it at all, to be at the moment before us: so does the Iliad: but *Faust*, and the *Genoveva*, and the *Laodamia*, and the *Ruth*, and the *Genevieve*, and the Dialogue between Tiberius and Vipsania, are beside it: whatever is imperishable, like the stars, or those poems, has never been young and never grows old.

New thoughts however... surely you must be very fond of them.

On the contrary, I would flee from them as from a hornet's nest; I would use more precautions against them, than against the bite of a tarantula: for the effect is not very unlike, only there is far more difficulty in finding out the music that will cure it. And I trust these volumes have all the appropriate symptoms of such a neophobia. I can wish for no higher praise of them, than that some thoughtful man familiar with the subjects about which they are chiefly conversant, should tell me he has long known everything they contain; known I say, not merely heard of. Nay, if I could ever aspire to produce a work which Wisdom should receive into her eternal archives, I know not whether my prayer would not be simply, that it might be full of ideas all at least as old as the Creation. In the sublime language of the great Giordano Bruno,

Si cum Natura sapio et sub Numine,
Id vere plusquam satis est. u.

Would anybody conceive it possible that the author of the foregoing lines, whose whole life and works were accordant with their spirit, should have been burnt for Atheism? None assuredly, except such as have mortified their souls by contemplating the atrocities which man hesitates not to commit, after he has once invested his Maker with his own diabolical passions. So unquenchable is man's hunger and thirst for religion, that, when no other God is set before him, he will deify even his own worst vices. When he is not called upon to worship in spirit and in truth, he will worship in lust and in blood. He will make his children pass through the fire to Moloch; his virgins must sacrifice their purity at the shrine of Mylitta; he will throw himself under the car of Juggernaut. And woe then unto him who would resist and cast down this idolatry! he is an infidel: he blasphemeth: he is an atheist: crucify him! crucify him!

It is remarkable that the men who have suffered persecution and death for atheism, have generally been the most godly of their age. Not only among the Jews did it happen, that such as were eminent for faith, through that faith and for that faith were tortured, had trial of cruel mockings and scourgings, of bonds and imprisonment, were stoned, were sawn asunder, were tempted, were slain with the sword. The Heathens were not much more tolerant of godliness. All the influence which Pericles had acquired among the Athenians by fair means and by foul, could not save Anaxagoras from banishment; and the troublesome piety of Socrates was silenced by a draught of hemlock. The Romans could let any doctrine pass, except that of Christ. Their descendants in after-times burnt Giordano Bruno and many others for atheism, because they were not sufficiently gross and carnal-minded: and Luther too would have been burnt for atheism, unless God had put it into the heart of the Emperor to keep his promise inviolate.

But such enormities could not be perpetrated in our civilized enlightened age.

Do you not know that light is nearest of kin to fire? O trust not in the efficacy of Civilization! there is no baser more senseless idolatry. It is with Civilization even as with the tree spoken of by the prophet: man burneth part thereof in the fire; with part thereof he eateth flesh; he roasteth roast, and is satisfied: yea, he warmeth himself, and saith, *Aha, I am warm, I have seen the fire*: and the residue thereof he maketh a god: he falleth down unto it, and worshippeth it, and prayeth unto it, and saith, *Deliver me; for thou art my god.* And was not Europe during the last century overrun by the priests of this idolatrous worship? all such regions of Europe at least as had brought to perfection the tree from which the idol was to be hewn. And was there not a like dearth of knowledge and understanding? to say *I have burnt part of it in the fire; I have baked bread upon the coals thereof; I have roasted flesh and eaten it: and shall I make the residue thereof an abomination? shall I fall down to it?*

Such was the state of Europe but yesterday: and if things are at all better today, it is not Civilization that has bettered them. As for any charm in Civilization to preserve us from cruelty, there is none such: if Civilization of itself could anywise soften the heart, it would be only by weakening and unmanning it: its fascination is like that of a serpent's eye, taking away all power of resistance. The uncivilized Athenians drove back into the sea the countless host of the Persians: the civilized Athenians crouched and fell before the army of the Macedonian.

> And may not we with sorrow say,
> A few strong instincts and a few plain rules,
> Among the herdsmen of the Alps, have wrought
> More for mankind at this unhappy day
> Than all the pride of intellect and thought?

It was among the outcasts from the civilization of Europe, the Russians and the Spaniards, that the latest enterpriser of universal empire foundered: wherever knowledge had taken its survey and drawn its charts, his course was easy; when he got into the unexplored regions of simple faith, unquestioning love of country, and devout loyalty, he ran aground. But weakness is often nearly connected with cruelty, as strength and courage are with kindness. 'He that is weak, is liable to fear; and fear is scarcely separable from hatred: painfully conscious of their own debasement, the feeble try to stifle that consciousness, when an opportunity presents itself, by an ostentatious display of all the mischief they can do. Fig-trees, which want a wall to lean against, like also to be manured with blood: oaks, which can support themselves, asking nothing of man save permission to shelter him with their majestic branches, draw their sustenance from the elements.

When Civilization is severed from moral principle and religious doctrine, there is no power in it to make the heart gentle. The Romans appear not to have been a ferocious or bloody people, until after they had been civilized; and the chief scene of the horrible atrocities which have recently polluted the earth, was the vain contemptuous self-sufficient capital of European Civilization, the Understanding's Unholy of Unholies. The humanizing influences of Civilization are manifested only when she is content to walk meekly among the handmaids of Religion: for Religion is the only true softener of the heart, Religion, when pure and undefiled, and encircled by the moral graces. Sophocles has beautifully exhibited this great truth, that Religion is the only inviolable sanctuary of the affections, by representing the heroic love of Antigone for her brother as springing from and upheld by her obedience to the " unwritten stable laws of the gods, which are not the birth of today or yesterday, but live from everlasting; and none can tell whence they were revealed."

The greater power of the affections over the modern world, is the most blessed earthly fruit which Christianity has borne; and if they are weaker now than they were among our fathers and forefathers, it is because they have been sapped by Civilization.

All who are read in the biographies of literary men, must feel assured that Knowledge of itself is anything but the parent of Charity. Knowledge gives an uneasy restlessness to the tongue, that unruly untamable evil, full of deadly poison. The very habit of conversing almost exclusively with our own thoughts, or with the speechless and lifeless thoughts of others as they lie in the intellectual burying-ground of a library, will too often indispose us for sympathizing with the living and breathing thoughts of our neighbours. When our thoughts are the main, if not the single, object of our thoughts, they naturally acquire a somewhat inordinate value. We become convinced that we are in the right, and so to a certain extent we ought to be: in intellectual as in all other action, nothing important or worthy can be accomplished without faith: but from faith one slides easily into bigotry: it is a very hard thing, to be convinced that we are in the right, without drawing the conclusion that all who differ from us must be in the wrong. Men are thus inclined to judge one another; he who judges may easily condemn; and before the hall of judgement stands the scaffold. Now this overweening presumption of the intellect is only to be kept down by religion, by the consciousness that our brethren are God's creatures, and that we are no more; so that whatever inequalities may exist among us in lesser things, in our highest of all relations, to the eye that looks down on us from heaven, they vanish. It is upon this principle that an apostle exclaims: *Who art thou that judgest another? there is one lawgiver who is able to save and to destroy*: and another apostle says in almost the same words:

Who art thou that judgest another man's servant? to his own master he standeth or falleth. Yea, he continues in the overflowing of his charity, *he shall be holden up: for God is able to make him stand.* But let man never wish to cast him down, whom God is able to hold up. u.

———

The worst of all monopolies is that which would monopolize God. u.

———

It is a gross and most mischievous, although a very common error, to represent religion as only the means and instrument of making men moral. Even the next step in the way downward is hardly more perilous, where morality is represented as only the means and instrument of making men happy, of producing an orderly and easy and pleasurable state of society. It is true, these effects will follow: godliness will make men moral, and morality will make them happy: but in neither case does the cause exist for the sake of the effect. It is necessary to distinguish between primary and mediate causes, those which produce effects either for their own purposes or after the order of nature, and those which are the mere implements in producing the effect, the shell out of which the kernel is to come. It is growing dark: I wish to see: I light my candles, by applying a burning match to them: it is evident that there are two causes of the candles being lighted; the primary, which is my wish to see; the mediate, which is the application of the match. Of these the latter is altogether subordinate to the effect; it exists solely for the specific purpose of producing such an effect, and having accomplished that purpose, it is cast away. But it is otherwise with the primary cause: that is not subservient to the effect; but the effect is subservient to it: nobody can say that I want to see, in order that my candles may be lighted; although such in the present state of things may be the natural result from that want. This is clear enough in all that is close at hand: so soon however as people begin to speculate about remote objects, they find the parts are not equally well defined; they cannot trace, so to say, the circulation of causality in the universe: it is much easier to go on in a straight line and then make halt: the difficulty in the chariot race, as Nestor enforces on his son, is to turn cleverly round the goal. When we find a cause habitually attended by any particular effect, we are fond of supposing that the effect is the cause of the cause; of which paralogism the dissertations on what are called final causes might furnish copious examples. The soul for instance lives not for the sake of animating the body, although the body is necessary for its earthly manifestation: but in the entanglement and thraldom of our senses, we readily believe our bodies to be the main portion of ourselves, to be, what in the Homeric age they were deemed, our real selves, as contradistinguished from our souls: the spirits of the heroes, says the bard, were hurled to Hades; their selves were a prey to dogs and birds. Nor again, although eating and drinking are necessary for the sustenance of the body, and so are the certain consequences of its existence, can the body be said to live for the sake of eating and drinking. Now morality is as it were the body of godliness, and is requisite for its earthly manifestation; it is the θρησκεία καθαρὰ καὶ ἀμίαντος spoken of by the apostle, without which all worship is vain: and accordingly perfect moral purity and perfect charity was, the form in which the Godhead became incarnate. Moreover as food is needful for the support and action of the body, so are empirical maxims of expediency for the developement and proper action of the moral principle. And since the bounty of God has connected pleasure with the fulfilment of whatever is according to his will; not only does the receit of food give pleasure, but also the discharge of duty. Man however has too often dissolved the union, by raising the lower above the higher, and, as it were, turning the vessel topsy-turvy: in both instances he has considered pleasure as the chief aim; he has thereby been led into intemperance physical and moral, and has disordered the constitution both of his body and soul.

The scale ascends then from expediency through duty to religion, not from religion through duty to expediency. Our earthly interests are at the bottom; our heavenly interests are at the top: they seem to be far asunder and almost incommunicable: but they meet and harmonize and atone in our duties; so that the moral law is as it were the interpreter between God and man. We seek diligently after that which is expedient, because it enables us to do that which is good, and thereby to manifest the beneficence of religion; not contrariwise. Nay, it is only when Expediency is impregnated more or less with the enthusiastic idea, the ἔνθεος ἰδέα of duty, that it can break its chain and escape from the kennel in which Selfishness couches growling at every passer by. The commonest household account cannot be cast up, without presuming the principles of arithmetic: neither can the motives for and against any action be cast up and balanced, without presuming the principles of moral arithmetic, that is, without reference more or less remote to some axiom of duty. Why am I not to get drunk? Because it injures my health? It will require an endless induction from particular cases to convince me of that: many of the healthiest men I know are among those who get drunk the oftenest: and it will be difficult to establish that anything but the sottish habit is mischievous, or that indulgence now and then does any harm at all. Because it is disgraceful? But the disgrace is a mere trifle: a toper is proverbially called a good fellow. And besides why is it disgraceful? except from a feeling more or less distinct of its being wrong: and why need I care about disgrace? where it is not likely to do me any sensible material hurt. Moreover you must shew me some pleasure to be derived from keeping sober, which shall overbalance the pleasure of getting drunk. But the moral law is explicit and peremptory: and nothing under the moral law can prohibit occasional transgressions. The moral law commands me undeviatingly to preserve the supremacy of my spiritual over my animal nature; it forbids me to drown my reason in wine: it commands me to be temperate in all things, in order that I may at all times possess the indefeisible mastery of my faculties. And why again am I to submit to such restraints? As the moral law has laid down the rule, religion supplies the principle: in order that my body and soul may be devoted without intermission to the worship of God; that, so far as in me lies, I may evermore have it in my power to employ them in some of those works of love, which are our reasonable and most acceptable worship. There is no denying the imperativeness of this command: there should be no resisting the efficacy of this principle. They both extend too over every particular case; while calculations of expediency drawn from consequences have no force save against habits: let offences come one at a time, and they will slip through: for to tell a man that one will make a way for another, is to insult his vigilance and self-command; and even the most timid will rejoin, that he knows best when to close his own gates. But the Stoic teacher arrived at the same conclusion with the Christian, that he who is guilty of a single tittle, is guilty of the whole law: only the Stoic knew of no way to wash off that guilt. For the degrees of sinfulness are of small significance, when compared with the exceeding sinfulness of sin, of turning aside from righteousness, of defacing the divine image in man, and, to use a word of Cudworth's, ungodding the soul.

Morality, I have said, is the outward form of Religion: the law is our schoolmaster to bring us unto Christ and make us the children of God, by renewing his image within us. Although the apostle is speaking with more immediate reference to the ceremonial law, the whole tenour of his argument here as elsewhere bears equally on the moral law; under which we continue, until being transfigured by faith we perform the works of the law in fulfilment of a more spiritual law, the living law of faith, compelling us by constraint not of fear but of love. It is thus that the Mosaic law was transfigured in the sermon on the Mount, and reappears there in a glorified form, another, yet still the same. Now the business of a schoolmaster is, not to spin a cobweb of rules in every vacant corner of his pupil's brain: such webs are of no use, except to catch flies, and to kill them: he should exhibit the rules as the skeleton which gives shape and firmness to the living particles surrounding and concealing it, as the form or mould in which the vital intelligent principle organizes the rude element of language: for a rule is only the residue of a fact distilled by the understanding, the footstep which a principle leaves behind it, to shew where its path has been; lasting indeed, and often gigantic as the footstep left by Hercules in Scythia, but no less undeserving of the worship which it too often receives. So also in the moral law ought we to look for something beyond the moral law, something more than the scaffolding for the construction of our conduct: we should endeavour to trace the flow of the religious principle through all the branching network of social life, and should thus convince ourselves that the highest and the true worth of morality, is its being the fittest mode of realizing godliness here on earth, in other words, its being the will of God. U.

Man is a parenthesis in nature. U.

It is in the heavens that we must read our way: without their enlightening guidance, the compass, useful as it may be in its subordinate department, will fail us when we are out in the midst of the broad shoreless sea. U.

Our life is a voyage.
Earth is our birth.
Heaven is our haven. U.

No science is so sure as Conscience. Science draws lines of circumvallation around Truth, to make it surrender, but generally only starves it. Conscience is seated within, in the citadel, and too frequently has to repel the attacks of Science. U.

Life ought to be the preliminary of peace: it is oftener employed in preparations for war; but still oftener in provoking and declaring war without any preparation. U.

Everybody seems to be persuaded that the author of the universe, like the author of the Iliad, aliquando bonus dormitat. U.

Nine times out of ten, the thing most agreeable in vice is that about it which is not vicious; at least not necessarily and confessedly. Enterprise, braving danger, avoiding an obstacle by contrivance or overthrowing it by a bold push, these are the things young men really love, when they fancy they love sin. But all these things may be enjoyed best in the craggy mountain-paths of virtue. There let them be sought. They will not prove less valuable for being unalloyed with evil.

A changeable creed is as absurd, as an unchangeable constitution.

Delenda est Carthago must be the motto of every moralist. To compromise with evil is to compromise the soul.

U.

Very many theological disputes and errors have arisen from the want of a clearly defined boundary between Belief and Faith. Mostly they are altogether confounded: yet they are exceedingly different. One is an act of the understanding; the other is a principle of the soul: and though they ought to be inseparable, they are very often severed. Faith may easily exist without being brought forward into that palpable insulated consciousness which is necessary to an act of belief: the most ignorant day-labourer has faith in the constant order of nature, and manifests it by making the whole course of his life conform to that faith: but he cannot be said to believe in the constant order of nature; for that article of his faith has never been set before him in the form of a distinct proposition. On the other hand nothing is commoner than Belief without Faith. It is common among the intelligent even here on earth; and we know that it is one of the attributes which characterize the diabolical nature: for the devils believe: they would not be devils if they did not: but the devils have no faith: they would not be devils if they had.

In other words, Faith is implicit Belief, and Belief should be explicit Faith: but in this world developement is often soon followed by dissolution; the leaves of the flower unfold, and drop off: and it is an idle endeavour to reproduce the flower by sticking them on again. u.

The postulate of Archimedes is as indispensable in metaphysics as in physics. In order to make any progress, one must have a given point to start from. He who begins nowhere, will never get on. What point you start from, matters less. There is hardly a spot on earth, whence a river, after it has once begun to flow, may not find its way to the sea.

Is it then to be supposed that in religion alone Knowledge can exist in a vacuum, and can know, without having anything given to it to know? Faith is the parent, not the child of Knowledge: although it is true that when Faith grows old or feeble, Knowledge, as is the duty of a child, may cherish and support her: if Knowledge contrariwise turns against and tries to slay Faith, as has sometimes happened, it is an act of parricide. When the apostle is describing the building of that spiritual man, whose headstone is charity, he makes him rest on the foundation of faith: he shall add to faith energy, and to energy, as the produce of the two, knowledge. For Faith to come from Knowledge is inverting the whole order of nature, according to which things grow out of darkness into light, and not out of light into darkness. This is beautifully expressed by Anselm in the sentences prefixed by Schleiermacher to his *Christian Faith*: Non quæro intelligere ut credam, sed credo ut intelligam. Nam qui non crediderit, non experietur, et qui expertus non fuerit, non intelliget.

Are we then to cast ourselves down into the desperate and abysmal belief that religion is unnatural to man? God forbid! Nothing is more natural: not light and sight to the eye; not the love of woman to the heart. As the eye is akin to light, and yearns for it, and rejoices in it; as the heart of man is not made to be alone, but feels, when woman is brought unto him, that she is bone of his bones and flesh of his flesh: so likewise is there something in his spiritual nature akin to God, something that yearns for and rejoices in his presence, that is not made to be alone, that when a divine truth is brought unto it, recognizes and acknowledges it and starts up to embrace it: there is a fountain of godly love that gushes forth like springing waters, when the earthy covering that shut it out from the light of heaven is pierced through. But as the eye cannot fashion the light that is to shine on it, nor make it shine, and, unless the light graciously shine on it, would slumber in dark obstruction, unaware of its own excellent nature; and as the heart of man although framed to love woman, cannot frame for itself the woman it is to love, and unless she be brought before it, will moulder in dreary apathy, unconscious of its beautiful capacities: so neither can the religious appetite in man create for itself the food it is to feed on: man cannot invent God; but he can know him, when he vouchsafes to reveal himself; and having once known God, can discover him in all things.

In the one sense then I believe there is

such a thing as natural religion; but not in the other sense, as devised and made by man himself. In its origin religion is supernatural; after it has once arisen, it becomes natural, inasmuch as it arouses and corresponds with that in man which is supernatural. υ.

Is it not a contradiction in terms, that a first cause or first principle should be demonstrated *à priori*? υ.

People accustomed to high living must have something new and recondite to stimulate their palled and cloyed appetites. Thus it is that we cannot see God, except in something marvellous and miraculous. Although it is in the order of the universe, inanimate and animate, unintelligent and intelligent, that the supreme Power and Wisdom and Goodness are most evidently displayed; so depraved and vicious is our taste, that the very constancy and universality of the manifestation hinder our observing it. If God were to grow faint and to slumber, and to let the universe droop and close its eyes and sink into the arms of sleep, we should then be aroused to perceive his being and his might: at present the power of God is hidden from us by his omnipotence.

A Parisian female philosopher exclaimed to some one who was explaining to her that everything in nature has its use: *Ah oui, pour la lune, elle est bien utile: elle nous éclaire pendant la nuit. Mais à quoi bon le soleil? qui ne se montre qu'en plein jour.* Well! we have all wit enough to laugh at her: but we have not wit enough to find out that her case is ours. For we too are continually blind to the presence and insensible to the love of God, because he is always and every where present, and because every breath of our bodies and of our souls is animated only by his love. We search after a source for the river, not for the sea. Nay, poor dull stupid senseless creatures that we are, we despise what is ordinary; we have even made it a by-word of reproach; and we disdain to be excited by anything but what is extraordinary. Savages perceive not God, except when he thunders and lightens. The prophet indeed, the man of God, when he stood before the Lord, and the Lord passed by, and a great and strong wind rent the mountains and brake in pieces the rocks, and after the wind an earthquake, and after the earthquake a fire, well knew that the Lord was not so immediately present in those exhibitions of destructive power, the wind and the earthquake and the fire, as in the still small voice, whether it be the still small voice of Law, which is the principle of the life of the universe, or the still small voice of Conscience, which is the principle of the life of the human soul. The man of God knew this: but an evil and adulterous generation seeketh after a sign. They cannot see God in the earth or in the heavens, in the alternation of night and day or the revolution of the seasons and all the blessings that drop from the wheel of Time as it circles; they cannot see him in the ebb and flow of life, throughout the world: but if they see a rod turned into a serpent, they are very willing to see him there. They cannot see the divinity of Christianity in all the good gifts which it has showered over the earth, in the dignity it has given to all the duties and hopes of man, in its answering every question of the soul and intelligibly solving the whole riddle of our being: but if they hear of a fig-tree withering, they are ready to fall down and worship. Nay more, many in this most idolatrous generation assert that the belief in such miracles is the only stable foundation for religious faith.

It was not thus that the Apostles preached. It was not thus that the great Christian philosopher Augustin taught. "The miracle (he says) of our Lord Jesus Christ, in that of water he made wine, is not to be marvelled at by those who know that God wrought it. For He made the wine on that day in those six water-pots which he commanded to be filled with water, who every year makes it in the vines. For as what the servants poured into the water-pots was changed into wine by the working of the Lord, so what the clouds pour down is changed into wine by the working of the same Lord. This however we do not wonder at, because it happens every year; by its constancy it has ceased to make us wonder. But who is there that beholds the workings of God, whereby this whole world is governed and administered, and is not astounded and overwhelmed by miracles. If he beholds the power of a single grain, of any seed, it is a mighty thing, it is awful to the beholder. But because men intent on something else lost the contemplation of God's works, wherein they should daily give praise to the maker; God, as it were, reserved to himself some unusual things which he might perform, that he might more wonderfully arouse men from their slumber to worship him. A dead man rose again: men marvelled: so many are born daily; and no one marvels. If we were to consider more reasonably, it is a greater miracle for him who was not, to be, than for him who was, to rise again. Yet the same God, the father of our Lord Jesus Christ, by his Word does all things and governs all things, who also created all things. The former miracles God wrought by his Word when with himself: the latter miracles he wrought by the same Word incarnate and made man for us. As we wonder at what was done by the man Jesus, so let us wonder at what was made by the God Jesus. By the God Jesus were made the heavens, and the earth, the sea, and all the glory of the heavens, and all the riches of the earth; and all the fruitfulness of the sea; all these things which lie before our eyes were made by the God

Jesus. And we behold them; and if his spirit is in us they so please us, as that we praise the maker; not so that turning to the work we turn away from the maker, and as it were turning our faces to the things made, turn our backs on him who made them. (*Exposit. in Evang. Johan. Tractat. VIII.*) U.

The whole life of Jesus was spent in giving alms. U.

We may well cry out against Absentees: we are crying out against the whole world. U.

I cannot pray. Then pray till you can. The most constant letter-writer has the most to say.

If things were as they ought to be, we should learn from Life to live, and from Death to die. But all is out of joint: the world is playing at cross purposes: and if we learn at all, it is rather

Death that teaches us to live, and Life that teaches us to die. u.

Every true Christian begins by committing suicide. u.

The history of the earth is a digression.
When will the subject be resumed?
At the day of Judgement. u.

It is awful to speak evil of the dead: and though *de mortuis nil nisi bonum.* would cut up history by the roots, yet he who delivered the maxim, feeling, as he must have felt at the moment of uttering it, what a thing Death is, how severing, how pitiful, how reconciling, spake well; and, if he only meant to inculcate as a moral duty abstinence from acrimonious or irreverent expressions against the departed and the dumb, I am quite sure that he also spake wisely.

exemplifies the unity of life, and blends its gayest with its most sorrowful scene, to have the same star heralding the night, which heralds the day. It leads us to perceive that day is only a brighter and more garish, and, unless it be tempered and sobered by solemn thoughts, a less worthy night; and that night is an expansion and higher power of day, wherein the finite vanishes in the infinite. The jollity of the bridal peal is softened and as it were veiled over by the thought of another world; and like the veiled bride herself it gives an intimation that there is something purer and more precious than the flaunting of earthly beauty: while on the other hand the sound of death loses somewhat of its ghastly hollowness, and may seem to be only the foreboder of a heavenly marriage.

U.

Death is the gate that leads from mortality to immortality. How indeed should a mortal become immortal except by casting off his mortality?

U.

What a beautiful thing a veil is! On passing from the North to the South of Europe, I know not what is more striking or more pleasing than the change in the female head-dress from bonnets to veils. The latter are not only surrounded with the glory of ancient association, having once overshadowed the brows of Grecian virgins and of Roman matrons, of Antigone and of Cornelia, while the approval of Saint Paul almost in a manner hallows them; but in themselves too they are incomparably more comely and more becoming. A veil is more flexible, more pliant, more graceful, and therefore more feminine: when the face is open, it hangs around it with a suitableness only to be surpassed by nature's own veil, the hair; which, as the Apostle tells us, was given to woman for a covering, so that, if it is long, it is a glory to her: when the veil covers the face, its folds mingle harmoniously with the folds of her other apparel, and it admonishes us that the wearer bears about her the mystery and the sanctity of womanhood. But bonnets are stiff, cumbrous, fantastical, grotesque, presumptuous, nay often, so perverse is fashion, shameless: they as it were impound our eyes on the flesh which they inclose: they strip the face of its appropriate back-ground, and thereby mar its picturesqueness: they bring out the full face with an effrontery that affronts, with a challenge of admiration which not seldom operates like a defiance: and although they are often made for the express purpose of shewing off the face, the whole face, and nothing but the face, they will sometimes enter into a daring and dangerous rivalry with it, and now and then stare it out of countenance, until the head seems to be a mere poll for shewing off the bonnet that tops it. Custom indeed, as it so often makes us blind to what is excellent, tends also to make us insensible of deformity: dislikes wear away, as well as likings: and the habits of our minds entertain a sort of fraternal affection for those of our bodies. Else how could such an animal as a fop exist in an age when dress is so unlovely and so graceless? Hence the only way of obtaining an impartial verdict, is, to give the cause a fictitious venue for the sake of bringing it before a less prejudiced tribunal. When we are looking at a picture, the judgement is not so likely to have been bruised or worn flat by use, or biassed by self-love: and we may be sure that whatever is ugly in a portrait, as a white waistcoat for instance, or a starched cravat, or a round hat, can never be truly handsome or seemly on a living form: although there may be extraneous notions of cleanliness or coolness or the like, which, together with habit, keep the eye from taking offence. Now between a veil and a bonnet, no painter could hesitate for a moment: the one welcomes his art; the other repels it. Still more decided, though perhaps less competent, is the sentence of Sculpture. Such of my readers too as have seen Madame Catalani at an Oratorio in one of our churches, cannot but have noticed the contrast between the chaste classical simplicity of the veil that overhung her fine features, and the gaudy peacocks' tails spread round the faces of our countrywomen: and few, I should conceive, can have had their taste so distorted by the confinement it had grown up in, as to doubt which was worthiest of preference, at least in such a place and on such an occasion. Which leads me to suggest by the way that the effect of those religious festivals would be greatly hightened and purified, if the female singers wore a simple, uniform, nun-like garb, more in accordance with the solemnity of the words they utter and of the buildings within which they utter them. Their dress now is strangely out of keeping with both. Above all things let them obey Saint Paul and wear veils. So should the eye help on the ear as it floats along the stream of sound, instead of retarding it, and distracting it, and filling it with its own unsatisfiedness and contrariety and confusion.

Even a plain face may be deemed fair behind a veil; and a lovely one loses little of its loveliness: that little too is abundantly compensated by the moral charms which breathe around it, and by the startling delight that attends its unforeseen undesigned manifestation. O that people would but bear this in mind! and would bear in mind also that, true as it is of sensuous beauty, it is still truer of moral beauty! Comely as every veil is, far comelier than any veil woven by earthly hands is the veil which modesty draws before genius, the veil which humility draws before goodness, concealing it not only from the eyes of others but from its own, and in very fact not letting the left hand know what the right hand doth. These are things the like of which one does sometimes see, albeit rarely, and perchance only in women. Men are induced by the practices, if not by the necessities, of life, to go bare-headed: their hat is only meant as a protection, to keep off the rain and wind and sunshine: and they seem to think that even in a spiritual sense, " if a man have long hair, it is a shame to him." A man's words and actions come down in large drops, with a hubbub, often causing a flood, often hardening into hailstones: a woman's, especially at that season of life when her mind's eye is beginning to see beyond the walls of her home, and her soul begins to feel that her own family, dear as they all are, yet are not enough to exhaust its gushing redundant affections, her fresh thoughts rise up like an exhalation, her kind deeds fall on you like dew; they cheer, they enliven, they gladden; yet you see them not; you hardly see whence they arise: no cloud precedes them, no noise accompanies them; the stars themselves cannot come forth more quietly: and the only change, if any, perceivable in her from whom they proceed, is, that she is somewhat less distinctly, somewhat more dimly seen. I have heard wisdom from men; but unfortunately they have generally known too well how wisely they were talking: the wisdom which I have sometimes imbibed from softer lips, has been far purer and more spiritual and more essential: it tasted not, like the other, of the cask: it wrought not by force, but by gentleness, nerving by softening, strengthening by comforting and rejoicing. With this veil thus encircling and clinging round the virgin soul, there is nothing in outward nature that can vie in loveliness; unless it be that etherial veil of light which the morning draws over the firmament: from which, by an image brought daily before our view, we may learn to frame some conception of the way in which Nature is the veil of God. And what if our senses are only such a veil drawn over our souls, concealing them, even as the daylight conceals the stars, supplying them with all the capacities needful for the uses and wants of our earthly being, and impenetrable, save by fleeting momentary glimpses, because to penetrate it would be to die! And what if Death be but a withdrawing of the senses from before the soul, as the evening withdraws the veil of light from before the stars; and a revealing of countless new realms of unfathomable incomprehensible being, to which those very senses now make us insensible! What if the sphere of Death be as far above the sphere of Life in magnitude, in grandeur, in wealth, in glory, and in sublimity, as the firmament of night surpasses the firmament of day! In our present state indeed we see only through a glass darkly: as we pierce through the film of daylight by the aid of a glass, so ought knowledge to be as a glass disclosing to us those spiritual and godly truths which are arrayed in the fair garment of Nature, and lurk behind her beautiful veil. Alas! it is oftener the glass which ministers to our lusts, or which helps us to gaze and wonder at ourselves. As for Truth, we are content to guess at it.

The veil which in the Temple divided the Holy place from the Holy of Holies, may perhaps be regarded as a type of this natural veil which conceals the supernatural world. The Epistle to the Hebrews indeed represents it as typical of Christ's human nature, the new and living way by which we enter into the Holiest. But types, as, were it needful, might easily be shewn, often admit of manifold interpretation: and at all events what was more immediately designed to typify the incarnation of the Word, may not unsuitably be looked upon as typifying the creation of the world by the Word. In one respect at least its applicableness cannot be questioned; and a diligent consideration of it would needs be very salutary: although the things which are not seen are most holy, the things which are seen are also holy, if we know but how to fix our eyes on them. The difference is not of contrariety, but of degree: we are already in the outer court: and it is our own fault if Death lead us not behind the veil, into the Holy of Holies. U.

There is but one tower "whose top reacheth unto heaven;" and man did not build it. Like the ladder seen by the patriarch, it was let down from above; and the eyes of faith may still behold the angels of God ascending and descending on it. We have still an Eden, if we will but enter it: for, as Stolberg says in his golden

Book of Love, " in the garden of the Scriptures too doth God walk, and would talk with man: but Adam hides himself amongst the trees." No Cherubim with flaming swords are placed there to drive us away; but the voice of Him who is higher than the Cherubim is evermore breathing from every part of it and calling us to come in.

Such as have loved to contemplate the reversal of the original curse, on seeing the name borne by the mother of sin as it were emblematically reversed in the first word of the hymn to the mother of the Saviour, on perceiving *Eva* reversed in *Ave*, may perchance find some food for their fancy in the similarity between *Babel*, the spiring fabric of pride, of the upstart attempt to take heaven by storm, converted by God into a spear wherewith to shiver the nations of the earth, and the *Bible*, the book of humility, the gracious summons and guide to heaven, the reveille of immortality, the cry of him who would gather all nations together even as a hen gathereth her chickens under her wings. Others will probably laugh at them. Be it so; provided they do it in mirth and gentleness: their pleasure may be somewhat like that of the former, although below it perhaps both in kind and degree. But let none laugh scornfully, for his own sake: the only person much harmed by scorn is the scorner. υ.

Nothing but the heavenly μῶλυ can save us from defilement and debasement in the den of Circe. True, it is a lowly herb growing out of the earth; but man cannot find it:

Χαλεπὸν δέ τ' ὀρύσσειν
Ἀνδράσί γε θνητοῖσι· θεοὶ δέ τε πάντα δύνανται.

The root too is black: it springs out of suffering and patience; but the flower is like milk, the milk of human kindness. υ.

Many men have been heroic in exploit; few

in endurance. Pride tells them that, to act, they must be doing something. And yet the greatest action in the whole history of the world is the Passion of Christ; an action almost as much surpassing all others in its heroic magnanimity, as it surpasses them in the extent and momentousness of its consequences. u.

Other religions take up their home in the past or the future; Christianity in the present, wherein the past and future are involved. That is, other religions are of Time, Christianity is of Eternity: for Time, it has been remarked, consists only of the past and the future; Eternity is always present. u.

One fine moonless evening under the influence of strong emotion I cast my eyes upward (I believe for sympathy) to the stars which were shining brightly above my head. But I felt that their heavenliness was too impassive for me, and became more conscious than ever of the necessity of an incarnation.

Love partakes of the infinite in its nature, and if it has not something infinite to feed on, feeds on and devours itself.

Living things are flexible in proportion to their life; and of all things the most flexible and plastic is the soul of man; just as, what was made for the soul, Christianity is the most flexible and plastic of institutions. Both of them indeed without violence to their nature may be adapted to anything but evil.

God unites opposites, because in him all things meet. God works by opposites, because from him all things issue.

Do you fancy yourself Phocion, that you attempt to drive men into conviction with such few arguments? To drive them into conviction? no: because in that case they would still be unconvinced. Our suggestions are only meant to lead people to set about convincing themselves. And for that purpose they can hardly be too brief. It is the same in that other great department of human action, war; for half the battle is to find our way, and the other half is to fight it. If you wish a general to be beaten, send him a ream full of instructions; if you wish him to succeed, give him a destination, and bid him conquer.

And so, Reader, (for it is time to have done with guessing) would I bid you conquer in your warfare against your four great enemies, the world, the devil, the flesh, and above all, that obstinate and perverse self-will, unaided by which the other three would be comparatively powerless. Many things in these pages may be mere guesses, crude and doubtful, hasty and remote from truth; but the chief things which they have pointed at, be assured, are not so; unless the earth be a guess, and the sun, and the sea, and virtue, and the word of God. These are so many beams of the same light, so many forms and manifestations of the one great presence that animates and upholds the universe, binding and embracing it with arms of love. He then, as the father and preserver and pervading life of all these wonderful realities, must himself be reality in the highest sense; nor can anything good be real apart from him. It is not I alone, nor any fallible man, who tell you this, but the visible witnesses of his existence, who are also the declarers of his will. Each has a voice of its own, and each is in unison with all. Listen to their universal chorus, and you shall hear it plainly say: *God is good; and we are good, for we obey God; and to obey God is to be good.*

And is this all? Yes, all perhaps that all

the varied voices of the universe distinctly utter; yet short as the lesson is, it will take us an eternity to practise. But how obey God? By striving to be what he is. For he evidently is our perfection; so that we must come nearer perfection in proportion as we approach to him. Strive then to resemble God; is he love? by cherishing love; is he truth? by studying to be like the truth, in your intellect by meditation, in your aims by single-heartedness, in your feelings by sincerity, in your actions by plain and open dealing.

I have set before you two great certainties; the Maker of the universe, and the duty of man. A third remains, the Bible, which declares and reconciles the preceding, and therewith instructs us in all needful knowledge, assuring us of a heaven at our journey's end, warning us against the enemies who will oppose our progress, and teaching us how, through whose intercession, with whose assistance, by what means, these enemies may be encountered and overcome. Yes! we shall triumph over them, dangerous as they are. For sin too is a reality, with its corrupting falsehoods, and their inevitable consequence, overwhelming final ruin. This is the real enemy against which you are summoned to contend. Range yourself against it under Christ's banner, nothing doubting; nor fly from the only field where to fight heartily is to conquer. God will himself do the rest certainly, if we will but certainly trust in him. His Grace and every other blessing be with you, Reader, and, if it may be, with the Guessers also.

Farewell.

THE END.

LONDON:
PRINTED BY S. AND R. BENTLEY, DORSET STREET.

June 1, 1827.

WORKS PREPARING FOR PUBLICATION,

OR JUST PUBLISHED,

BY JOHN TAYLOR, WATERLOO-PLACE,

And sold by JAMES DUNCAN, PATERNOSTER-ROW.

I.

A TRANSLATION of the forthcoming Second Edition of NIEBUHR'S ROMAN HISTORY: undertaken in concert with the Author by the REV. JULIUS C. HARE, M. A. Fellow of Trinity College, Cambridge, and CONNOP THIRLWALL, ESQ. M. A. Fellow of Trinity College, Cambridge. *In the Press.*

This Second Edition is now in course of publication in Germany:—in the mean time the Author forwards the sheets as printed to England, and will himself contribute Corrections and Additions to the Translation.

The Author writes to a friend in England, that he is anxious it should be known as early as possible, that this New Edition is not a Reprint of the Old Work with Additions and Improvements, but absolutely a New Work, in which few pages of the former have been retained.

II.

TWELVE POPULAR LECTURES on the STEAM ENGINE, explaining, in a very short compass, the structure and operation of that Machine, as adapted for various purposes, in a style suited to those who are unacquainted with Mechanical or Mathematical Science. These Lectures will also contain a Sketch of the most striking and important circumstances in the HISTORY of the STEAM ENGINE. Illustrated with Cuts. By the

New Works published

Rev. DIONYSIUS LARDNER, LL.D. of Trinity College, Dublin, F.R.S.E.; Hon. F.P.S. CAMB.; F.AST. S.L.; Hon. F.S.A. SCOT.; M.R.I.A., &c. &c. *In the Press.*

III.

A new Edition of the FIRST SIX BOOKS of EUCLID'S ELEMENTS, with a Commentary, General Demonstrations, Geometrical Exercises, &c.; to which are annexed, THE ELEMENTS OF SOLID GEOMETRY, abridged from the Eleventh and Twelfth Books; adapted for the use of schools and Under-graduates in the Universities. Edited by the REV. DIONYSIUS LARDNER, LL.D. &c. &c. *In the Press.*

IV.

The TRAVELS of MIRZA ITESA MODEEN, in Great Britain and France. Translated from the original Persian, by JAMES EDWARD ALEXANDER, Esq. late Lieutenant of his Majesty's 13th Light Dragoons. With a Portrait of the Mirza, 1 vol. 8vo. 9s.

V.

The same Work in English and Hindoostanee, 8vo. 18s.

VI.

A LETTER TO A RELATION.
" Yet a little while the light is with you. Walk while ye have the light, &c. JOHN xii. 35. Foolscap 8vo. 1s.

VII.

The SHEPHERD'S CALENDAR, with VILLAGE STORIES and other Poems, by JOHN CLARE, author of " Poems" and " The Village Minstrel," Foolscap 8vo.; with a Frontispiece, engraved by E. Finden from a Drawing by P. De Wint. 6s.

VIII.

The SCIENTIFIC LIBRARY: a Series of Elementary Works on the Sciences. By GEO. DARLEY, A.B.—comprising *for John Taylor, Waterloo-Place.*

Vol. 1st. A SYSTEM OF POPULAR GEOMETRY, containing in a few lessons, so much of the Elements of Euclid as is necessary and sufficient for a right understanding of every art and science in its leading truths and general principles. Price 4s. 6d.

Vol. 2d. A SYSTEM OF POPULAR ALGEBRA. Price 4s. 6d.

Vol. 3d. containing **POPULAR TRIGONOMETRY** and **LOGARITHMS**, with the application of Algebra to Geometry, *is in the Press.*

IX.

V. **A SYSTEM of CLASSICAL INSTRUCTION**, combining the methods of LOCKE, ASCHAM, DEAN COLET, and others—containing

1. **VIRGIL'S ÆNEID**, Book I, on Locke's Interlineary Plan. Price 2s. 6d.

2. **PARSING LESSONS** to the same, with a short Latin Grammar.

3. **HOMER'S ILIAD**, Book I. Interlinear. Price 2s. 6d.

4. **PARSING LESSONS** to the same, with a short Greek Grammar.

5. **CÆSAR'S INVASION of BRITAIN**, Interlinear, with Notes, &c. *In the Press.*

6. **THE ODES OF ANACREON.** Interspersed with Notes, &c. *In the Press.*

X.

AN ELEMENTARY TREATISE on the Differential and Integral Calculus. By the Rev. DIONYSIUS LARDNER, LL.D. 8vo. 21s.

XI.

AN ANALYTICAL TREATISE on PLANE and SPHERICAL TRIGONOMETRY, and the Analysis of Angular Sections. By the Rev. DIONYSIUS LARDNER, LL.D. 8vo. 12s.

XII.

A CRITICAL ESSAY on the GOSPEL of St. LUKE, by Dr. FREDERICK SCHLEIERMACHER: with an Introduction by the Translator, containing an Account of the Controversy respecting the Origin of the Three First Gospels, since BISHOP MARSH's Dissertation. 8vo. 13s. boards.

XIII.

The LABOURS of IDLENESS, or Seven Nights' Entertainments. By GUY PENSEVAL. Contents: Epistle Dedicatory.—1. The Enchanted Lyre.—2. Love's Devotion.—3. Pedro Ladron, or the Shepherd of Toppledown Hill.—4. Aileen Astore, or the Glen of the Grave.—5. The Dead Man's Dream.—6. Ellinore.—7. Lilian. Post 8vo. 9s. 6d. boards.

XIV.

SONGS of SCOTLAND, Ancient and Modern; illustrated with Notes, a Critical Introduction, and Characters of the most eminent Lyric Poets of Scotland. By ALLAN CUNNINGHAM. 4 vols. post 8vo. 1l. 16s. boards.

XV.

IS THIS RELIGION? or a Page from the Book of the World. By the Author of "May you like it." Foolscap 8vo. 7s. boards.

XVI.

AIDS to REFLECTION in the FORMATION of a MANLY CHARACTER, on the three Grounds of PRUDENCE, MORALITY, and RELIGION, illustrated by Extracts from the Writings of the Elder Divines, especially from Archbishop Leighton. By S. T. COLERIDGE, Esq. Post 8vo. 10s. 6d. boards.